I have known Mark for many years ana ne is faithful, authentic, passionate, honest and kind. I commend both the author and his book to you.

MIKE PILAVACHI (SOUL SURVIVOR)

Personal, perceptive, profound, provocative, well-resourced and well-written; Mark Bradford offers us an imaginative and encouraging exploration of encounter as the key and critical mode of Christian experience and discipleship.

THE RT REVD JAMES BELL (BISHOP OF RIPON)

The stories in this book may be familiar, but we are offered a fresh insight. The journeys travelled by early disciples are fleshed out for a contemporary eye.

THE RT REVD NICK BAINES (BISHOP OF LEEDS)

This book takes you deeper into the Easter story by exposing the failures and successes, doubts and certainties, and above all the unashamed humanity of the cast of characters who follow Jesus to the cross and beyond.

JILL ROWE (OASIS ETHOS & FORMATION DIRECTOR)

Connecting theology with experience, and mission with spirituality, Mark offers a careful reading of the New Testament encounters with Jesus, leading us into experiencing the transforming power of the resurrection for ourselves.

IAN PAUL (THEOLOGIAN, WRITER AND SPEAKER: WWW.PSEPHIZO.COM)

Reading Mark's unfolding of the risen Christ, we are challenged to put the resurrection at the centre of who we are as Christians as well as what we do. This will orientate us to a discipleship that holds together death and new life, so we can know the victory of Christ without ignoring the reality of suffering.

CHRISTINA BAXTER (FORMER PRINCIPAL, ST JOHN'S COLLEGE, NOTTINGHAM)

Text copyright © Mark Bradford 2016
The author asserts the moral right to be identified as the author of this work

Published by
The Bible Reading Fellowship
15 The Chambers, Vineyard
Abingdon OX14 3FE
United Kingdom
Tel: +44 (0)1865 319700
Email: enquiries@brf.org.uk
Website: www.brf.org.uk
BRF is a Registered Charity

ISBN 978 0 85746 428 6

First published 2016
10 9 8 7 6 5 4 3 2 1 0
All rights reserved

Acknowledgements
Unless otherwise stated, scripture quotations are taken from The Holy Bible,
New International Version (Anglicised edition) copyright © 1979, 1984, 2011
by Biblica. Used by permission of Hodder & Stoughton Publishers, an Hachette
UK company. All rights reserved. 'NIV' is a registered trademark of Biblica.
UK trademark number 1448790.

Scripture quotations from The New Revised Standard Version of the Bible,
Anglicised edition, copyright © 1989, 1995 by the Division of Christian Education
of the National Council of the Churches of Christ in the United States of America.
Used by permission. All rights reserved.

Scripture quotations taken from the Holy Bible, New Living Translation, copyright
© 1996, 2004, 2007, 2013. Used by permission of Tyndale House Publishers, Inc.,
Carol Stream, Illinois 60188. All rights reserved.

Scripture quotations from the Good News Bible published by The Bible Societies/
HarperCollins Publishers Ltd, UK © American Bible Society 1966, 1971, 1976,
1992, used with permission.

Scripture taken from THE MESSAGE. Copyright © 1993, 1994, 1995, 1996, 2000,
2001, 2002. Used by permission of NavPress Publishing Group.

'Seven Stanzas at Easter' by John Updike. Copyright © John Updike 1964, used
by permission of The Wylie Agency (UK) Limited.

'Pentecost' by R.A. Wright. Copyright © R.A. Wright, used by kind permission.

Cover photo: Lindrik/Thinkstock.com

Every effort has been made to trace and contact copyright owners for material
used in this resource. We apologise for any inadvertent omissions or errors,
and would ask those concerned to contact us so that full acknowledgement
can be made in the future.

A catalogue record for this book is available from the British Library

Printed and bound by CPI Group (UK) Ltd, Croydon CR0 4YY

Encountering the
Risen Christ

From Easter to Pentecost:
the message of the resurrection
and how it can change us

Mark Bradford

One suggestion for using this book would be to read it throughout the seven weeks of Easter. In this way, the first chapter would be read in the week following Easter Sunday, while the last would be finished in time for Pentecost Sunday.

Contents

Seven Stanzas at Easter

Make no mistake: if He rose at all
it was as His body;
if the cells' dissolution did not reverse, the molecules reknit,
*   the amino acids rekindle,*
the Church will fall.

It was not as the flowers,
each soft spring recurrent;
it was not as His Spirit in the mouths and fuddled eyes of the
*   eleven apostles;*
it was as His flesh: ours.

The same hinged thumbs and toes,
the same valved heart
that—pierced—died, withered, paused, and then regathered
*   out of enduring Might*
new strength to enclose.

Let us not mock God with metaphor,
analogy, sidestepping, transcendence,
making of the event a parable, a sign painted in the faded
*   credulity of earlier ages:*
let us walk through the door.

The stone is rolled back, not papier-mâché,
not a stone in a story,
but the vast rock of materiality that in the slow grinding of time
*   will eclipse for each of us*
the wide light of day.

And if we will have an angel at the tomb,
make it a real angel,
weighty with Max Planck's quanta, vivid with hair, opaque
    in the dawn light, robed in real linen
spun on a definite loom.

Let us not seek to make it less monstrous,
for our own convenience, our own sense of beauty,
lest, awakened in one unthinkable hour, we are embarrassed
    by the miracle,
and crushed by remonstrance.
JOHN UPDIKE (1932–2009)

– Chapter 1 –

Introduction

Jesus said to her, 'I am the resurrection and the life' (John 11:25).

There is only one qualification needed to experience resurrection: to be dead.[1]

There is a profound difference between a 'meeting' and an 'encounter'.

Meetings are usually planned and predictable events. Encounters are often unplanned and can have consequences far beyond anything that we can imagine. Meetings tend to be fairly superficial affairs in which the 'usual business' is discussed. Encounters are deep affairs in which the agenda is not set by us. We can often walk out of meetings largely unaffected by what has happened. We are unlikely to leave an encounter unchanged. In fact, we may never be the same again.

This was certainly the case for Mary, the disciples as a group, Thomas, Cleopas and his companion, and Peter—as we will explore in these pages. And it was also the case for a young man named Saul.

Saul (or, as he later became known, Paul) set out on a journey from Jerusalem to Damascus. He knew who he was and he knew what he was about. Saul had an immaculately defined sense of identity and one that, at least before he encountered the risen Christ, he was deeply proud of. He was a pure-bred Jew, who could trace his ancestry for 2000 years, right back to the patriarchs Abraham, Isaac and Jacob. He even knew from which of Jacob's sons he was descended—it was Benjamin. To be able to know such a thing gave Saul a great sense of honour and prestige—in the way that a blood connection with royalty or celebrity might today. Saul was circumcised, the sign of belonging for the male Jew, traditionally performed on the eighth day. Furthermore, as a Pharisee, he prided himself on the way in which he kept the law. Like his ancestry and his circumcision, this was a sign of his deep purity as a Jew. Saul, as far as he was concerned, was 'blameless' (Philippians 3:4–6). Far from merely living all this out in his own private world, Saul was fighting for the purity of Israel on a wider stage.

Saul was a man on a mission, consumed with zeal like the great defenders of the faith in years gone by. More specifically, he was determined to eradicate a new religious group, known as 'the Way', which was emerging in and around Jerusalem. For him, this new group was becoming a distraction, even a threat to the beliefs that he held so strongly. In his black-and-white world, such a situation could be tolerated no longer.

Saul is first mentioned in the Bible in the context of the execution of Stephen, the first Christian martyr. Stephen was a member of this new sect and was described as being 'full of God's grace and power' and doing 'great wonders and signs among the people' (Acts 6:8). In an act of jealousy, some members of the local synagogue stirred up the people against Stephen and brought false reports about him in order to bring him before the Sanhedrin, the Jewish Council. Stephen's defence was a brilliant exposition of how Jesus, the very man they had killed on that first Good Friday, was in fact the culmination of their own long and proud story of faith going all the way back to Abraham. Safe to say, this did not go down well, and Stephen was dragged outside the city and stoned. The witnesses to this act laid their coats at the feet of a young man named Saul, and Luke, the writer of the book of Acts, makes it clear that Saul approved of their killing Stephen (Acts 8:1).

Following the martyrdom of Stephen, the followers of Jesus became scattered throughout Judea and Samaria as persecution broke out against the church in Jerusalem. Ironically, though, this only served to spread the news of Jesus further and wider than before. Where Saul had previously gone from house to house, dragging off men and women to be put into prison (Acts 8:3), he now had to cover a far larger circuit in order to contain the spread of these people who were talking about Jesus as Messiah. In order to do this, he went to the high priest in order to ask permission that he might round up any who, like Stephen, were followers of the Way. Though he did not yet realise it, Saul was fighting against a force far greater than even his own zeal and passion. Unlike his own teacher, Gamaliel, he had not considered the possibility that this new religious group might have divine, rather than human, origins, and that, as a result, he might find himself fighting against God (Acts 5:35–39)! Saul hadn't factored in the reality that the whole world—in fact, the whole cosmos—had changed forever as a result of the events of that first Easter weekend.

It would take Saul some time to catch up with this reality. And so it does still for us today.

Introduction to Easter

Easter has always been the high point of the church year. This can often be difficult for us to appreciate because the society around us tends to get far more excited about Christmas than Easter. And yet, as far as the Christian story is concerned, it is Easter, and not Christmas, that is pivotal. Christmas is significant, of course; but Easter is decisive. As Tom Wright remarked: 'Take Christmas away, and in biblical terms you lose two chapters at the front of Matthew and Luke, nothing else. Take Easter away, and you don't have a New Testament; you don't have a Christianity.'[2] THE MESSAGE paraphrase of 1 Corinthians 15:14 captures Paul brilliantly on this: 'And face it—if there's no resurrection for Christ, everything we've told you is smoke and mirrors, and everything you've staked your life on is smoke and mirrors.'

Basically, if nothing happened at Easter, we should pack up and go home because there is no 'Christianity'.

But if something *did* happen at Easter, then it changes *everything*.

This is what Christians have always believed—that something extraordinary, remarkable, unrepeatable, *did* happen at Easter. And so this event, and only this event, can form the zenith of the church's marking of sacred time. For it was this event that established Jesus Christ as the Son of God in power; as the Lord of the world. And it is on the basis of this event that assurance has been given to the world that God will one day judge the world in righteousness. No wonder, then, that the first apostles in the book of Acts saw themselves as witnesses to the resurrection of Jesus and that the heart of their message—which would land them in so much conflict with the powers of the day—was to teach and proclaim 'that in Jesus there is the resurrection of the dead' (Acts 4:2, NRSV; see also Acts 1:22; 17:31; Romans 1:4).

Early Christian sources reveal distinct modes of celebrating Easter.[3] However, the one that became universal was to keep the feast on the Sunday following the Passover, and to focus the celebration upon the resurrection of Jesus Christ from the dead, which, according to all four canonical Gospels, had taken place on the first day of the week. Yet, from as early as the second century, a number of sources indicate that the celebration of Easter took place as a 50-day *season*, rather than merely a day. Paul Bradshaw writes, 'It was regarded as a time of rejoicing, and every day was treated in the same way as Sunday, that is, with no kneeling for prayer or fasting.' Some called the 50 days of Easter 'one great Sunday', while every Sunday in the year was considered a little Easter in which to celebrate the whole story of redemption.

Yet, in my experience, the contemporary church has, in practice at least, lost a vital sense of the importance of Easter. Lent is often kept, with plenty of resources around for this 40-day period preparing us for Easter. Of course, such a season can be of great benefit in stripping back our lives, in freeing us from our multiple addictions, to ensure that we are holding fast to that which is truly important. The excitement builds from Palm Sunday and into Holy Week, before the foreboding events of Maundy Thursday, the darkness of Good Friday and the silence that is Holy Saturday, and we eventually reach the triumph that is Easter—Christ victorious, death defeated, grave denied! But somehow, inexplicably, we only celebrate this for a single day. And yet, as I've said, Easter in the church calendar is not just a single day; it is a whole season. And where Lent was 40 days long, the Easter season is 50. The energy put into our self-denial during Lent should be far outstripped, both in intensity and longevity, by the energy put into feasting and celebration during Easter. Chaplain Mike observes well the lack of imagination around the practice of the season of Easter:

Shouldn't Easter Sunday unleash a season of festivity unlike any other? Shouldn't it bring a time of celebration unmatched by any other season? Why is there not a flood of Easter music? Why not an entire season of feasting, rejoicing, doing good works, showing generosity, practicing hospitality, giving gifts, engaging in special mission and service projects, holding sacred concerts and art festivals, and decorating our homes, churches, and communities with beautiful reminders of new life and hope?…

But it's not just what we do (or don't do) when we get together this time of year. It's the lack of theology, the lack of in-depth discussion, the lack of consideration, contemplation, and immersion in resurrection life that I'm missing in me and all around me. What **difference** *does it make that Jesus is alive and seated at the right hand of the Father?*[4]

I have a feeling that this is not simply a matter that concerns our worship and celebration, but, intrinsically, also something which detrimentally affects the quality of our discipleship and mission. For it is not just who or what we worship that shapes us, but also how and when. Thus, the church very often misses what Easter, resurrection, and new creation mean in practice and how they affect everything concerning what it means to follow Jesus. I spoke recently to a friend who had spent her life in churches where she was continually told that she needed to 'die to herself'. This is all well and good but, by itself, it had left her with a very negative view of herself. What she had not been given the chance to hear was the invitation, in Christ, to be raised to new life—with new hope and new possibilities at work, both in her and through her. A message of crucifixion emphasised above resurrection, of Good Friday above Easter, is really no message at all. But tragically, all too many contemporary understandings have tended to swing towards this extreme.

So what does the surprising reality of Easter and the wonder of the resurrection actually mean for the church? For creation and the cosmos? For me?

Perhaps it is time for us, like Saul, to encounter afresh the risen Christ.

The nature of an encounter

In any encounter with the risen Christ, there are perhaps at least three stages to journey through: as for Saul, so for us.

1. Disorientation

The first stage of any encounter is that of disorientation— for our known worlds to be called into question. This sounds harsh, and yet, as the Greek philosopher Epictetus observed not long after Saul, 'it is impossible for anyone to begin to learn that which he thinks he already knows'. For Saul, a man so full of conviction and certainty, of zeal and confidence, it would be a dramatic event. Perhaps it had to be this way for him.

Saul was journeying along the road, coming to the edge of Damascus—ready to complete his mission—and then, suddenly, there was a flash of light from heaven. He fell to the floor and a voice began speaking to him: '"Saul, Saul, why do you persecute me?" "Who are you, Lord?" Saul asked. "I am Jesus, whom you are persecuting," he replied. "Now get up and go into the city, and you will be told what you must do"' (Acts 9:4–6). For Saul, calling all the shots, and deciding exactly what would be done to whom in Damascus, this must have been a hugely disorientating experience. Suddenly he was not in control any more; someone else was calling the shots. Saul was unable to see for three days—a man of zealous vision, suddenly rendered blind. More alarming still, this person calling all the shots said that he was 'Jesus', who Saul would have known all about.

Saul would have known that Jesus was a prophet, with claims to be the Jewish Messiah, but that he had been crucified and buried not long before. And, of course, Saul would have heard the claims of the early followers of Jesus that, in fact, this Jesus had not stayed dead but had been raised to life again. Yet Saul was having none of it, and was doing all that he could to root out such absurd claims. Quite simply, a crucified Messiah was a failed Messiah. And, besides, Jesus' 'resurrection' was all wrong. The hope of Israel at this time was for resurrection, but, crucially, it would be corporate—for all of Israel—and it would come at the end of the age. Jesus simply did not fit into these expectations: his was a resurrection happening to one person in the middle of time. Saul had no categories in which to fit such an understanding of resurrection. So he did what we all do: he sought to eradicate whatever did not fit into his preconceived understanding.

For Saul to be able to journey forwards—not so much towards Damascus but in terms of his understanding of God and his purposes in the world—he had first to be brought to his knees. For him to truly be able to see, he first had to be blinded. For a new world to come into view, his known world had first to be levelled, with everything he had built his life on to this point called into question. Encountering the risen Christ would do all these things for Saul, and an encounter with the risen Christ can be equally disorientating for people today.

Many churches leave feedback cards for visitors to fill in with questions, notes, prayer requests and the like. One church in California received the following feedback one Sunday: 'I was enjoying a cup of coffee with some members of your church and when the music started I followed them inside. What a shock! Songs about Jesus, stories about Jesus, prayers to Jesus. It was like I had walked into some creepy Jesus cult. You do know he's been dead for 2000 years, right?'

How we all need reminding—not least those of us in the 'Jesus cult'—that he isn't dead; he is alive! How we need the unexpected to disorient us, to blow us off course, to call into question our current way of living. How we need a fresh encounter with the risen Christ. Easter was the most genuinely surprising event the world has ever seen. We cannot turn the power of this, nor our walking with the risen Christ, into something predictable. Christ is always reliable, but he is never predictable. We need always to be open to the ways in which he will seek to disrupt the usual business of our lives. Disorientation is so important, because the older we get, the more set in our ways we tend to become. We commit ourselves to a particular path and, once committed, it can be hard to change course.

This is really what the Christian term 'repentance' is about: changing course; unlearning in order to relearn. As Alvin Toffler has pointed out, 'The illiterate of the 21st century will not be those who cannot read but those who cannot learn, unlearn and relearn.'[5] And yet, our own stubbornness aside, another obstacle to unlearning and relearning is the pace of modern life itself. As the pace of life becomes faster and faster, there is barely enough time to do, let alone to think, reflect and consider whether we are walking the right way. We may be aware of the sadnesses, the fears, the questions, the failures and the shattered dreams that we carry around with us, like baggage on our backs, but we have no time to consider what we might do with them.

Sometimes, the only way that God can get through to us is to bring us to our knees. To stop us in our tracks. To bring us to a point where life simply doesn't make sense any more; and we need to pause, to reflect on the disorientation, and then to reimagine other possibilities. We need to realise that we are 'dead' and in need of resurrection.

2. Reimagination

If an encounter with the risen Christ is like an explosion, then its purpose is to blast away the old and to clear some space in which to reimagine God, Jesus, the world, oneself—everything! The encounter on the road to Damascus was that explosion for Paul, forcing him to reimagine everything he had previously held as central. In fact, he had to spend the next few years of his life reworking previous understandings. When he came to write to the Philippian believers, he was able to say:

If anyone else has reason to be confident in the flesh, I have more: circumcised on the eighth day, a member of the people of Israel, of the tribe of Benjamin, a Hebrew born of Hebrews; as to the law, a Pharisee; as to zeal, a persecutor of the church; as to righteousness under the law, blameless. Yet whatever gains I had, these I have come to regard as loss because of Christ. More than that, I regard everything as loss because of the surpassing value of knowing Christ Jesus my Lord. (Philippians 3:4–8, NRSV)

This is reimagination on an epic scale—everything that was previously profit now written off as loss. Paul's encounter with the risen Christ did indeed change everything for him.

The standard Jewish way of viewing the world—to which Paul certainly adhered—was that there was one God (monotheism), one people chosen by God to bring blessing to the world (election), and one future for the world (eschatology). And yet on each of these counts, in the light of the explosion that was his encounter with the risen Christ, Paul had to rethink and reimagine utterly his whole way of viewing the world and living within it. His belief in one God, so vital in preventing a fall into idolatry, had to be rethought around Jesus and the Spirit. Thus, as early as Paul's letter to the Galatians—which is one of the earliest Christian documents we possess—Tom Wright notes, 'One might conclude that if the doctrine of the Trinity had not come into existence it would be necessary to invent it.'[6]

The sense of being part of the chosen people of God had to be expanded around the work of Christ in his death and resurrection such that now, 'there is neither Jew nor Gentile, neither slave nor free, nor is there male and female, for you are all one in Christ Jesus' (Galatians 3:28). The ground is truly level at the foot of the cross; divisions that once held sway have now been smashed down. Finally, there was a realisation that God's future for the world had, in Christ, come forward into the present. Resurrection, expected for all at the end of time, had happened in the middle of time for Jesus. The renewal of all things would still wait to the end for its final consummation, yet there was a realisation for Paul, because of Easter as well as the ascension, that Christ is already reigning, and with him the people of God too.

In the light of his encounter with the risen Christ, Paul profoundly reimagined everything that made up his life and his worldview.

We are invited to do the same—to see the world in an entirely different light, with all that we carry around with us through life. In the ground cleared by an encounter with the risen Christ, is there space to reimagine our sorrows, our fears, our doubts, our sense of failure, and our shattered dreams? What does the fact that Jesus died but rose again mean to us in each of these areas? Where have we stopped imagining new possibilities for our lives and convinced ourselves that the 'old script' is the only one that has the potential to shape us?

As we look at the encounter of Mary Magdalene with the risen Christ (Chapter 2), we will see that she was invited to journey with him from sadness to hope.

As we think about the disciples in the upper room (Chapter 3), we see that Jesus meets them in their fear and invites them towards a place of confidence.

Through the story of Thomas (Chapter 4), we see someone with doubts and questions whom the risen Lord Jesus beckoned towards a fresh encounter through which his faith was confirmed.

In the journey of the two disciples towards Emmaus (Chapter 5), we see two people whose dreams were shattered but who, through an encounter with a stranger in word and action, found the opportunity for a new beginning.

In Peter we see someone who dramatically failed Jesus (Chapter 6), but who found in an encounter with the risen Christ both forgiveness and restoration.

What was possible for all of them is equally possible for us, as we encounter the same risen Christ. Christ meets us where we are and invites us to journey with him, from our brokenness and toward his wholeness.

3. Transformation

The test of whether one has truly encountered the risen Christ is always in terms of transformed living.

Paul's experience of disorientation and reimagination was never about abstract theology, divorced from the reality of life. Rather, this was the very frame of reference into which he would live and minister for Christ. Paul, always a man on a mission, would take on a very different mission from the one that he had been embarking on before the Damascus road experience. The most passionate and pure-bred of Jews would become the apostle to the Gentiles. The one-time persecutor of the church would suffer immense persecution for Christ—though he would see this as participating in Christ's own sufferings, on the way to gaining resurrection life himself (Philippians 3:10–11). And, according to Christian tradition, this would eventually lead to him losing his life— like his master, obedient unto death—although, in Paul's mind, this really meant gaining his life and being with Christ.

Sometimes I think we can get stuck on this one. So many of our approaches in church gatherings, of one sort and another, are typically information-heavy—think sermons, Bible studies, courses, conferences, even this book! Now, of course, there is a place for all these things; but sometimes it can feel as though we are saturated with information but sorely lacking in transformation. Mahatma Gandhi, the pre-eminent leader of the Indian independence movement in British-ruled India, once said: 'I like your Christ, I do not like your Christians. Your Christians are so unlike your Christ. If the Christians lived their gospel, there would be no more Hindus in India.'[7] Were he still alive today, what would his judgement be on today's church?

Contrast this with the following description of Christians in the second century:

Christians cannot be distinguished from the rest of the human race by country or language or customs. They do not live in cities of their own; they do not use a peculiar form of speech; they do not follow an eccentric manner of life... Yet, although they live in Greek and barbarian cities alike, as each one's lot has been cast, and follow the customs of the country in clothing and food and other matters of daily living, at the same time they give proof of the remarkable and admittedly extraordinary constitution of their own commonwealth. They live in their own countries, but only as resident aliens. They have a share in everything as citizens, and endure everything as foreigners. Every foreign land is their fatherland, and yet for them every fatherland is a foreign land. They marry, like everyone else, and they beget children, but they do not cast out their offspring. They share their food with each other, but not their marriage bed... They love all people, and by all are persecuted. They are unknown, and still they are condemned; they are put to death, and yet they are brought to life. They are poor, and yet they make many rich... They are reviled, and yet they bless; when they are affronted, they still pay due respect... To put it simply: What the soul is in the body, that Christians are in the world.[8]

These early Christians stood out from those around them. They were a part of society; yet they had a distinctive way of living. For example, in an ancient society in which excess babies, especially baby girls, were taken to the local 'landfill' to die of exposure, Christians went to the rubbish dumps to rescue them and then to raise them as their own children. Furthermore, these Christians also shared their possessions; they didn't take revenge when they were attacked; they were buoyant even when they were persecuted. They had encountered the risen Christ as a living reality in their own lives and their lives were transformed as a result.

This begs the question as to how truly different Christians are from those around them today. We may believe different things from our friends and family who are not Christians, but how radically distinctive are we in the way that we live out our lives? Dallas Willard refers to the modern curse of 'barcode Christianity', in which people affirm Christian belief—as though hoping to receive an invisible barcode that God scans at the entrance of heaven to determine who can enter—and yet remain unchanged both on the inside and in how they conduct their lives.[9]

And yet one thing is certain: encountering the risen Christ truly changes people.

Just think about Paul. He was the persecutor of the church who became a planter of churches. The man who had once sought to tear the church apart became someone who gave everything physically, emotionally and spiritually to build it up; the one who approved of the killing of Christians became one himself, and is likely to have been martyred for his faith (probably in Rome around AD66 during the persecution under Emperor Nero). That's quite some turnaround.

The same is true of Mary, Thomas, Peter, the couple on the road to Emmaus, and the disciples as a whole—all were radically changed. They moved from sadness to hope, from fear to confidence, from doubt to confirmation, from failure to restoration, and from shattered dreams to new beginnings.

But this wasn't about an invitation to some kind of therapeutic fulfilment. In a consumer age, there is always the danger that we will interpret Jesus' promise of 'life in all its fullness' (John 10:10, GNB) as simply a Christian version of the consumer dream in which we are given health, wealth and all we could ever hope for. On the contrary, in the words of Dietrich Bonhoeffer, 'When Christ calls a man, he bids him come and die.'[10] For, as Jesus had said, 'Whoever wants to be my disciple must deny themselves and take up their cross and follow me. For whoever wants to save their life will lose it, but whoever loses their life for me and for the gospel will save it' (Mark 8:34–35). In the same way that Easter Sunday was only possible because Jesus walked the way of Good Friday, so the journey to sharing in Christ's resurrection life cannot come to us any other way than through faith and baptism and being prepared also to share in his death. For many of the early disciples, and for many disciples of Jesus today, this can mean martyrdom. However, at the very least it means being prepared for this, and walking a whole new way, whatever happens.

In New Testament times encountering the risen Christ changed people. He is still in the business of changing people today.

Pause and reflect: 'Prayer of St Brendan'

St Brendan the Voyager reputedly set sail from Ireland in the fifth century in a small coracle made of wood and oxhide, and ended up in Newfoundland. His story, and the prayer below, inspire us to journey into disorientation, reimagination and transformation with the risen Christ.

Take some time to pray slowly through this prayer:

Lord, I will trust You;
help me to journey beyond the familiar
and into the unknown.

Give me the faith to leave old ways
and break fresh ground with You.

Christ of the mysteries, can I trust You
to be stronger than each storm in me?

Strengthen me with Your blessing
and appoint to me the task.

Teach me to live with eternity in view.
Tune my spirit to the music of heaven.

Feed me,
and, somehow,
make my obedience count for You.[11]

Discussion questions

- Do you think we over-celebrate at Christmas and under-celebrate at Easter? How could we celebrate Easter as a season rather than simply a day?
- Would you say that you know who you are and what you are about? Is it a good thing or a bad thing to know this?
- Can you recall a moment where you have felt 'disoriented' in your faith? Was this a good or a bad thing?
- What might limit our ability to reimagine?
- Why do you think that transformation is often such a slow process for us?

– Chapter 2 –

Mary: Sadness and Hope

Weeping may stay for the night, but rejoicing comes in the morning (Psalm 30:5b).

He that lives in hope danceth without music (English proverb).[12]

Barbara Johnson, in her book *Splashes of Joy in the Cesspools of Life*, has described Christians as 'Easter people living in a Good Friday world'.[13] We do not need to look too far around us—nor too far within ourselves—to understand the tension that this phrase evokes. The resurrection of Jesus Christ has unleashed new life into the world, and this new life is known in, and through, all those who have been raised in Christ, by faith and baptism. However, this new life has both *come* and is still *yet to come*. In the midst of surprising new vitality, we remain confronted with darkness and pain and death. The bridge between our sadnesses and the joy of the new creation to come is the dynamic of hope, which can only be founded upon the good news of Easter and known by an encounter with the risen Christ. This was the story for Mary.

Now Mary stood outside the tomb crying. As she wept, she bent over to look into the tomb and saw two angels in white, seated where Jesus' body had been, one at the head and the other at the foot. They asked her, 'Woman, why are you crying?' 'They have taken my Lord away,' she said, 'and I don't know where they have put him.' At this, she turned round and saw Jesus standing there, but she did not realise that it was Jesus. He asked her, 'Woman, why are you crying? Who is it you are looking for?' Thinking he was the gardener, she said, 'Sir, if you have carried him away, tell me where you have put him, and I will get him.' Jesus said to her, 'Mary.' She turned towards him and cried out in Aramaic, 'Rabboni!' (which means 'Teacher'). Jesus said, 'Do not hold on to me, for I have not yet ascended to the Father. Go instead to my brothers and tell them, "I am ascending to my Father and your Father, to my God and your God."' Mary Magdalene went to the disciples with the news: 'I have seen the Lord!' And she told them that he had said these things to her. (John 20:11–18)

Mary: from sadness to hope

Mary was a close friend and follower of Jesus. In Jesus, she had found deep freedom and great liberation (Luke 8:2; Mark 16:9), but she had also been there at the awful moment of his crucifixion. Here, Mary stands outside Jesus' tomb in deep sadness. She has come early on the Sunday, while it is still dark—a metaphor of a revelation that hasn't yet dawned—to find the stone rolled away and the tomb empty. She has been to inform Peter and John, 'the other disciple, the one whom Jesus loved', and they have come to see for themselves. However, now they have gone, and Mary is left, weeping.

She looks into the tomb and sees two angels there, sitting where the body of Jesus had been. They ask her the obvious question as to the reason for her weeping, and Mary gives the obvious answer—the fact that some people have taken Jesus away, but she does not know where. The first question, the first answer, and now the first turning, as Mary turns to see Jesus standing there—the same Jesus who, not long before, had wept at the loss of a friend and visited his tomb (John

11:35)—although she does not yet know that it is him. As we will see throughout this book, there is a mysterious quality to the risen Christ. He can be seen but not fully recognised. It is only through encountering him that we truly come to see him for who he is.

The stranger-Jesus repeats essentially the question of the angels—again, asking the reason for her weeping, and who it is she is looking for. The irony of the question is tangible: the one she is seeking is stood right there in front of her, encountering her before she has even realised that she is encountering him. And following the second question, she gives her second response—that she wants Jesus to tell her where Jesus has been laid, so that she can take care of his body! John's Gospel often shows people getting the wrong idea—and so here, it is revealed that Mary sees the man in front of her, not as Jesus, but as a gardener. Of course, in a sense she is right—this is Jesus, the new Adam, the gardener, charged with overcoming the chaos that had entered the garden of Eden (Genesis 3), taking the thorns and thistles, and all that they represented, as a crown upon himself. So Mary, even though she is wrong, is right, but she cannot understand all of that yet.

As with all the post-resurrection encounters, there is an incredible sense of drama to this story. I love the sense of recognition that dawns on Mary as Jesus speaks her name. Anyone could have spoken her name, but there must have been something about the way that Jesus said it that stopped her in her tracks. The other words that Jesus had spoken hadn't caused the light to dawn on her—but when he said 'Mary', the illumination became clear. Maybe no one ever said Mary's name quite like Jesus did.

But now, this is what the Lord says—he who created you, Jacob, he who formed you, Israel: 'Do not fear, for I have redeemed you; I have summoned you by name; you are mine.' (Isaiah 43:1)

How does Jesus speak my name? Your name? And do we recognise his voice when he does?

I write these words just two days after the Church of England has consecrated its first female bishop—Libby Lane as Bishop of Stockport. The journey for the Church of England to reach that point has been long and arduous, painful and complex. Yet for those, like myself, who support the full ministry of women, this encounter of Mary with Jesus is perhaps one of the strongest pieces of biblical support. Mary is the first to see, meet and speak to the risen Jesus. She is the first apostle—the first person 'sent out' with the good news of Jesus. She becomes 'the apostle to the apostles' (John 20:18), as she goes and tells that she has seen the Lord and what he has said to her.

Stories are most often seen as credible when there is something within them that is so unlikely and implausible that they simply have to be true. One common daily prayer for Jews of the day would have been 'Blessed are you, O God, King of the Universe, Who has not made me... a Gentile, a slave, and a woman.' On a similar note, according to the Jewish law of the day, the testimony of a woman counted for precisely... nothing! So when God does the most incredible, the most unbelievable thing in the history of the world, and when he wants to announce it so that all will believe, whom does he choose to witness to such an event? That's right, a woman! God is in the business of reversing the way in which things happen in the world.

As the apostle Paul would later observe:

But God chose what is foolish in the world to shame the wise; God chose what is weak in the world to shame the strong; God chose what is low and despised in the world, things that are not, to reduce to nothing things that are, so that no one might boast in the presence of God. (1 Corinthians 1:27–29, NRSV)

We know that women played an integral part in spreading the 'good news' in the early years of the church, because of the contrast in how Jesus' female followers were treated before and after his resurrection. At the time of Jesus' crucifixion, the men ran away—fearing for their lives—whereas the women could move around freely, because revolutionary movements were for the men and the women stayed clear. However, in Acts 22:4, Paul makes it clear that he persecuted those belonging to the Way—an early name for Christians— putting both men *and women* in prison. The women were now seen as just as dangerous as the men.

Mary and the disciples: disorientation and reimagination

The hope that Mary and the disciples came to find in Jesus is at first perplexing. Everyone knew that a crucified Messiah was a failed Messiah. How then to make sense of a crucified but apparently resurrected Messiah? Mary can only speak to the disciples of what she has seen and heard (v. 18). Thus, initially there is only disorientation. The events of this first Easter weekend were not fitting into the preconceived mindsets that were available for the disciples' thinking. In Christ, God had done something completely new, altogether surprising, deeply unpredictable. Hence, the need for reimagination. Mary and the disciples had been expecting a Messiah who would triumph by inflicting suffering and death on the enemy. They would soon come to see that Jesus had triumphed over the enemy, but by taking suffering and death upon himself.

The problem was that, at the time, the Roman occupiers were seen as the problem. But Rome was merely the symptom of a far wider disease, that of sin and suffering and death. And just as a good doctor would not think she had done her job by merely alleviating a few symptoms of a pandemic disease, so Jesus knew that he would go far deeper and further than those around him would have imagined. Though he was the only one not to be part of this pandemic, he had to take the disease upon himself, allow it to do its worst to him in claiming his life, but then in his death to exhaust its virulence and, by the power of God's Spirit at work in him, overcome it and rise to new life. Only then was he able to offer immunity, an antidote, to the disease for all who would put their confidence in him.

In light of this, what the Messiah has accomplished is more than could ever have been envisaged. Exile has been ended—not only the exile situation of having pagan Roman power in the land, but the wider exile from Eden. Jesus is the gardener, the new Adam, who has taken the thorns and thistles upon himself and overcome their power so that new creation can come.

The shape of the Christian hope

Over the past decade or so, I have benefited greatly from the writings of N.T. (Tom) Wright in helping me rethink what Easter and Jesus' resurrection really mean in a broader theological context. Brought up on a 'gospel message' that, put crudely, said, 'Jesus came to die so that we could go to heaven when we die', I have come to see that what happened to Jesus on Easter Sunday is, in fact, the prototype for what will happen to all who are followers of Christ when he appears to judge and renew the world.

1 Corinthians 15 is clearest on this, and in this chapter Paul says that Jesus' resurrection represents the 'firstfruits' of those who have already died (1 Corinthians 15:20–23). Paul deliberately takes up this word 'firstfruits' as an allusion to the Jewish holiday that had the same name. God commanded the people of Israel to offer the 'firstfruits' of their harvest to him on the first day following the sabbath of Passover (Leviticus 23:9–14). In a sense, this was a sacrifice of faith—faith that, if God had already provided the nation with a bountiful initial harvest, then the people could anticipate with confidence an even more bountiful harvest in the coming months. In the same way, Jesus' resurrection gives God's people hope that we too will experience the same bodily resurrection that Jesus experienced, in the future. Jesus' resurrection is not simply a historical event, but also a foretaste of what is to come in the future, when God gives us new, redeemed bodies. We live today in the light of all that happened on that first Easter Sunday, and in anticipation of the day when all things will be renewed. And yet, we know that we live in a world in which, despite the cataclysmic events of Jesus' resurrection, there is still so much hurt, pain, suffering and death. We are Easter people living in a Good Friday world. The firstfruits are here, but the full harvest has not yet come.

As we will see, there were some things about Jesus' body which seemed to be similar to his body before resurrection:

he ate and drank, so he clearly wasn't a ghost; people touched him. Yet there were also some differences: his appearance, while eventually recognisable, was different, as shown by the number of times people initially failed to know him; also, he came and went seemingly at whim; locked doors were no barrier to him. We can only imagine what this will mean for our bodies.

God will give us, in the end, resurrection bodies because we will be living in a renewed world. Jesus' resurrection is not only the prototype for a renewed humanity but for a fully redeemed creation. The view I grew up on was that 'heaven is my home' and we are simply 'passing through' this world, on the way to something greater. In this view, there can be a marked separation between the sacred and the secular, the spiritual and the physical, the higher and the lower, the eternal and the temporal. However, a more thoroughly biblical approach places a proper stress on God as the creator of the heavens and the earth; the creator of all things. So, in the words of a famous hymn by M.D. Babcock, 'This is my Father's world'.

When God created the world, he said that it was 'good', and we know that God hates nothing that he has made. So God will not dispose of creation, but rather renew it and restore it to all that it was meant to be. When we read passages such as Romans 8, we hear not only of human beings but also creation itself groaning for redemption. It's also what we find when we look at, in my view, one of the most incredible passages in the whole Bible—Revelation 21—in which it becomes clear that, in the end, it won't be us who change our address but God who changes his. There will be a new heaven and a new earth; the holy city—the dwelling place of God—comes down to us; we don't go towards it. In this place God will be where he has always wanted to be—at home with the people of his creation—and he will wipe away every tear from our eyes. Death will be no more; nor will grieving or crying or pain because the old creation has gone and the new has come. Sadness will be gone forever; joy will be eternal, because hope has been fulfilled. Easter is but a foretaste of that.

Sadness and hope today

A new world is coming, but it has not yet come. The simple reality of death in our world means that we, like Mary, may find ourselves grieving at the loss of a loved one—enduring the painful reminder that creation, for all its beauty, is broken. Death is the ultimate symptom of a chaos that has its roots much deeper.

In late 2010 and early 2011, my dad had a number of seizures. Initially these were put down to epilepsy, and medication was prescribed accordingly. At first, this seemed to be keeping the issue at bay, but three days after his discharge from the consultant, he had a fourth and then fifth seizure. An MRI scan diagnosed a brain tumour which was removed as far as possible in surgery but which proved to be malignant and fast-growing. Despite radiotherapy and chemotherapy, my dad died in North Devon Hospice on 11 November 2012. During his illness and death, I went through the different stages of grief—denial, anger, bargaining, depression and acceptance, according to the pioneering Swiss-American psychiatrist Elizabeth Kübler-Ross—though my passing in and out of them was erratic, unpredictable, and sometimes spectacularly emotional. Someone once said that grief is the price we pay for love; it is love that is now homeless, with no place to go. I was well supported by family and friends. However, I did observe that some Christians, instead of just listening or even sitting with us in painful silence, felt the need to resolve their own discomfort with glib sentiments like 'Everything happens for a reason' or 'Don't worry, he's gone to the great party in the sky.' I'm not sure I do believe that everything happens for a reason; yes, God is sovereign, but there remains a whole lot of chaos in the world, as yet unresolved. The second comment, while true, was hopelessly ill-timed. What I needed first was empathy, not eschatology.

Yet eschatology is so important. There is grief—deep, painful grief—and yet for those who are in Christ, we do not 'grieve as others do who have no hope' (1 Thessalonians 4:13). Death is only sleeping, because in his resurrection, Jesus Christ has conquered death and drawn from the grave its sting. There need be no fear of death. There will be sadness, but sadness will not have the final word. As Jesus said, when he raised his friend Lazarus from the tomb: 'I am the resurrection and the life. The one who believes in me will live, even though they die; and whoever lives by believing in me will never die' (John 11:25–26).

Hope beckons us to look forward to the day when the dead in Christ will be raised and the whole of creation made new. Meanwhile, if we take a simple look round at the wider world, we see that this day has not yet come.

The 20th century began with 'the war to end all wars' and yet turned out to be the most murderous in recorded history. Though the nature of warfare may be changing, the 21st century shows little sign thus far of being any more peaceful. Meanwhile, across the world, the gap between the rich and the rest is growing faster than ever. The richest 85 people on the planet have as much wealth as the poorest half of the global population. And this increasingly extreme inequality is destabilising economies, damaging societies and pushing more people into poverty. In a country such as the UK, we might think that we are immune to such issues. However, food banks are on the rise in the UK and one in five people live below the poverty line, with life expectancy in some areas lower than in some developing countries. In fact, the UK is on course to become one of the most unequal countries in the industrialised world.[14] Though technological advances and the advent of the digital age mean that our society is more connected than ever before, paradoxically many people are more alone. This is not only an issue among older people, as might have been expected, but is growing among younger people too.

Among Christians, there can be two, equally unhelpful, responses to such problems. One is to stand and point the finger in judgement ('look how bad our society is becoming!'), most likely with a link to the inevitable consequences of that society turning its back on God. Yet the job of judging is not ours. There is one judge, Jesus Christ, who has been entrusted with the role by God the Father. We should leave the judging to him. Second, however, we may be tempted to try to save society. Overly confident in our own (self-) righteousness, the church can act as though we have all the 'answers' which simply need to be imposed on the wider world and then all will be well. If the church is a negative presence in its judging of society, it can be a downright dangerous one when it gets the bit between its teeth on some aggressive moral crusade. Again, the church is not the saviour of the world; Jesus Christ is. Resisting messianic zeal, however well-intentioned, is just as vital as refusing to stand in judgement. I believe that the first call of the church in relation to the wider world is neither to judge it nor to save it, but rather to weep over it.

Even before we do this, we must first weep over ourselves. We must always seek change in ourselves before we can do it in others, because, as Richard Rohr would remind us, what we do not transform, we transmit. Before we can seek to tell the truth about the world around us, we must first be prepared to admit the truth about ourselves. This is difficult for a number of cultural reasons. First, we are taught always to see ourselves as the victim, and never the perpetrator of anything. Everything is always 'someone else's fault'; blame is always external rather than internal. Second, there is so little concept of 'sin' any more, for in many ways we have become a post-sin society. Sins are simply things that are 'naughty but nice', a bit like the 'syns' on a dieting programme.

I am currently in the process of being led, by a very wise Zimbabwean monk, through the Spiritual Exercises of St Ignatius. Sometimes the language and world can feel overly medieval, and in need of just a little translation. However, what I have most appreciated so far is the way in which the exercises seek to take sin seriously. The second exercise in the first week is pretty demanding. Part of it is the following: 'I will call to mind all the sins of my life, reviewing year by year, and period by period. Three things will help me in this: First, to consider the place where I lived; secondly, my dealings with others; thirdly, the office I have held.' As a prelude to this: 'to ask for what I desire. Here it will be to ask for a growing and intense sorrow and tears for my sins.' Just as Mary came to the tomb and wept, so participants are invited to reflect on the tomb-like places of their lives and to weep. Aleksandr Solzhenitsyn, who was imprisoned for eight years for criticising Stalin, wrote, 'The line separating good and evil passes, not through states, nor through classes, nor between political parties either, but right through every human heart, and through all human hearts.'[15]

The purpose of such a reminder as this is not guilt, but contrition; not beating oneself up, but falling on one's knees before God. Everything is not all right in us, and we should not pretend that it is. However, the exercise does not stay in sadness but resolves itself in wonder and hope. Wonder that God is merciful and forgiving, and hope that we can be changed more and more into the likeness of Christ.

Such 'high-bar' approaches to the Christian life are rarely found in the comparative comfort of the modern church, though they are to be found in places. Howard Astin of St John's, Bowling, Bradford, has written a very challenging book, *12½ Steps to Spiritual Health*,[16] in which he takes the 12-Step programme to deal with drug or alcohol addiction, and applies it to our addiction to sin. The first step, though, is to admit that we have a problem, an addiction, in the first place. Again, this is not to say that everything that happens is my fault, but that I am caught up in the mess that pervades and fills the world around me. I am not immune from it. Such an understanding of myself can only make me humble about who I am, and compassionate in my treatment of others.

As we look at the world around us, this compassion is first expressed in grief, tears, weeping. This world is our home, and yet the present arrangement of the world is *not* our home. As Mary came to the tomb, the symbol of a broken creation, so we stand at the broken places of our world and weep. Where is there suffering, brokenness and death affecting those around us—our friends, our families, our churches—that God would call us to weep over? Part of the answer in Mary was that she was prepared to linger; to be present to that place of pain and suffering, and not run away from it. She stood there, initially at least, wordless.

When we take in the news of the wider world, and as we are confronted daily by the horrors of famine, homelessness, injustice, violence, war, inequality, and so much other pain and suffering, we so often feel we do not have the words. But that is the point, we don't have the words. I used to have no way of praying if I didn't have the words; somehow, I didn't think that my prayers would be effective if I was unable to articulate what I was thinking. Thankfully, I have come to an awareness that I am praying most deeply and most profoundly when I do not have the words. Romans 8 speaks of a creation that is groaning, out of kilter, longing for its redemption. It also speaks of a God who is not distant from this groaning creation but, in fact, is deeply present to it. But the way in which this God is present is through the Spirit as the Spirit groans in the people of God—not only for their redemption but also for the redemption of the world. As Paul says, 'the Spirit helps us in our weakness; for we do not know how to pray as we ought, but that very Spirit intercedes with sighs too deep for words. And God, who searches the heart, knows what is the mind of the Spirit, because the Spirit intercedes for the saints according to the will of God' (Romans 8:26–27).

The strongest prayers are the weakest ones; the most profound prayers are the ones when we do not know what to say, because God's Spirit is crying out within us, beyond the power of words. Thus, beyond the power of words we just need to be present, to linger, both in our prayer for others and in our care for them.

Such intercession is only possible because there is hope.

Everything is not all right in the world around us. And yet, because of the resurrection of Jesus Christ, we believe that a new world is coming, and so we pray in anticipation of that new world in the present: 'your kingdom come, your will be done, on earth as in heaven'. However, we must not only pray for the world in hope, but must also proclaim to the world that there is hope. Such proclamation will be done with our words and with our lives. Having encountered the risen Christ, we, like Mary, must tell of what we have heard and of what he has done. As Thomas Merton has said: 'Eschatology is not an invitation to escape into a private heaven: it is a call to transfigure the evil and stricken world.'[17] C.S. Lewis agrees:

If you read history you will find that the Christians who did most for the present world were those who thought most of the next. It is since Christians have largely ceased to think of the next world that they have become so ineffective in this world.[18]

This is why the National Church and Social Action survey indicates that over a million volunteers participated in church-based social action in the UK in 2014, touching millions of people through various initiatives.[19] These include activities such as community building (for example, parent and toddler groups); compassion ministries (for example, caring for the elderly); crisis intervention (such as debt advice); and education (such as school assemblies). Levels of volunteering among churches are on the increase, as are the levels of financial giving that sustain such projects. As Lord Wei of Shoreditch commented in relation to the report:

It is inspiring to see over a million Christian volunteers across the UK engaged in community social action day in and day out. This is the Church 24/7 building community, comforting in distress, helping in crisis and demonstrating Christian values. We should applaud their example and recognise and support their efforts.'[20]

We should take great encouragement from such reports. And if we struggle to believe that *we* could really make a difference, we need to remember the old African proverb: 'If you think you are too small to make a difference, you haven't spent the night with a mosquito.'

A new world is coming. In prayer and presence, we lean into it, in anticipation of that day when his kingdom *has* come and his will *is* done on earth just as it is in heaven.

Pause and reflect: 'This is my Father's world'

Sadness and hope; prayer and presence. This is what it means to be an Easter people living in a Good Friday world—bridging the gap between the two; uncomfortably, awkwardly at times. It is hard to express this better than in the words of a verse from the hymn mentioned above:

This is my Father's world.
O let me ne'er forget
That though the wrong seems oft so strong,
God is the ruler yet.
This is my Father's world:
why should my heart be sad?
The Lord is King; let the heavens ring!
God reigns; let the earth be glad![21]

Discussion questions

- How have you understood 'life after death' in the past? What difference does it make if we understand it in the ways spoken of in this chapter?
- Why do you think people today can be so uncomfortable around the issue of death? Have you seen in practice what difference it makes to have encountered the risen Christ and to have to face this issue?
- How much sadness do you feel over your own sin?
- Have you ever experienced grief while you have prayed for someone or something?
- How, in practice, can we be bearers of the message of hope that Easter celebrates?

Chapter 3

The Disciples:
Fear and Confidence

But Jesus immediately said to them: 'Take courage! It is I. Don't be afraid.' (Matthew 14:27)

Jesus promised his disciples three things: to be absurdly happy, completely fearless, and in constant trouble. (F.R. Maltby)[22]

We live in a world of fear; we are afraid of so many things. And we are tutored and encouraged in our fears by so many powers in our world: the media, politicians and advertisers, as well as many others. But Jesus comes to set us free from our fears, because 'There is no fear in love. But perfect love drives out fear' (1 John 4:18). His resurrection marks the triumph of love over fear—and for all who are in him, there is no need to be afraid. Instead, we stand on his resurrection in a place of confidence and security. How funny, then, that we are afraid of making known the good news of his resurrection! How funny that Christians down the ages have lost their lives for making known that news, but we can so often be so afraid of simply losing face in front of people. And yet how deeply comforting to know that we are not the first disciples to be afraid of such a thing—that, in fact, the very first disciples were afraid of precisely this. Maybe, as they were changed in their encounter with the risen Christ, so we can be too.

The disciples encounter the risen Christ

On the evening of that first day of the week, when the disciples were together, with the doors locked for fear of the Jewish leaders, Jesus came and stood among them and said, 'Peace be with you!' After he said this, he showed them his hands and side. The disciples were overjoyed when they saw the Lord.

Again Jesus said, 'Peace be with you! As the Father has sent me, I am sending you.' And with that he breathed on them and said, 'Receive the Holy Spirit. If you forgive anyone's sins, their sins are forgiven; if you do not forgive them, they are not forgiven.' (John 20:19–23)

Just as, in the *The Lion, The Witch and The Wardrobe*, the coming of Aslan heralds the end of winter and the dawning of spring, so now with the death and resurrection of Jesus Christ, new life has come to the world. Again, John stresses that it is 'the first day of the week' (v. 19), to re-emphasise that this is a new Genesis moment, a new creation moment. All sorts of fresh and unexpected things are happening. Or in the words of Song of Songs 2:11–13a:

See! The winter is past;
the rains are over and gone.
Flowers appear on the earth;
the season of singing has come,
the cooing of doves
is heard in our land.
The fig-tree forms its early fruit;
the blossoming vines spread their fragrance.

The disciples have not yet caught up with the coming of spring. They are still living in the deep pangs of winter. They are meeting together, but they are doing so in fear that the path of the Teacher—suffering and crucifixion—will also become the path for them as his disciples. At this time, that is a path they are not prepared to walk. The doors are locked, as a means to help them feel 'safe', but I imagine this was of little comfort in truth. The room will have been heavy with the atmosphere that comes when troubled minds and anxious hearts are united in fear. And so, just as Mary's 'sadness' needed to play catch-up with the 'hope' of the resurrection, so the 'fear' of the disciples needs to be caught up, overtaken, and overwhelmed in the 'confidence' that comes from encountering the risen Christ.

John states, in a very matter-of-fact way, that 'Jesus came and stood among them' (v. 19), and yet he's only just told us that the doors were locked. Clearly things that were restricted, locked down, access denied, in the old world, can now be transcended in the new. This is a world of new possibility for those who have the eyes of faith, rather than of fear, to see. As Karl Barth said: 'Christ does not remain outside knocking, waiting for us. The risen Christ passes unconditionally through closed doors.'[23]

And Jesus speaks some words to them: 'Peace be with you.' In my church, we share these words each week as a prelude to sharing the Eucharist together. 'The Peace' was announced in a service only last week, and a new lady to our congregation muttered under her breath, 'What on earth is "The Peace"?!' For many, it is a series of awkward handshakes and half-smiling moments with a series of different people sat around you. As far as the word 'peace' in English is concerned, very often it can simply be viewed as 'the absence of conflict'—a sort of vacuous, neutral state where simply nothing bad is happening. However, in the biblical sense, it stands for so very much more.

The Greek word for 'peace' (*eirene*) comes from a root which means 'to join, tie together into a whole'. Peace in this understanding is about all the essential parts of something being joined together into a whole. This is what the writer of the letter of Colossians is saying has happened through the death and resurrection of Jesus Christ—that in Christ, the broken pieces of the world have been put back together again. I particularly love *THE MESSAGE* paraphrase of Colossians 1:19b–20:

Everything of God finds its proper place in him without crowding. Not only that, but all the broken and dislocated pieces of the universe—people and things, animals and atoms—get properly fixed and fit together in vibrant harmonies, all because of his death, his blood that poured down from the cross.

This Greek word picks up on one of the most profound words in the Hebrew scriptures—that of *shalom*. Again, this word has a wealth of meaning that lies far beyond an anaemic sense of 'a lack of conflict', instead denoting 'well-being' in its widest possible sense. It incorporates notions of contentment, health, prosperity, justice, unity and salvation, and functions at all possible levels of life—individual, communal, national, international, and creational (compare Psalm 4:8; Isaiah 11:6–9). And, because God is the creator of all things, and because everything that he made was 'good', God's desire is the healing and restoration of his creation, and not its destruction, nor our escape from it. Hence those phenomenal words above from Colossians 1: 'all the broken and dislocated pieces of the universe—people and things, animals and atoms—get properly fixed and fit together'.

So, when Christians share 'the Peace', if that is part of their tradition, this is a profound thing—celebrating the *shalom* that we have, because of all that Christ has done, both with God and with one another, and anticipating the day when creation will cease its groaning, when God will redeem all things, and finally he will be 'all in all'.

Having pronounced 'peace' on them, Jesus then 'showed them his hands and side' (v. 20). This is undoubtedly one of the most fascinating aspects of the resurrection for me— that the risen Jesus still bears the wounds he received on the cross. They weren't erased. They weren't healed in the way that many of us probably would have had it, had we been writing the script. In turn, this calls for reflection on what we understand by the notions of 'wholeness' and 'perfection'; and how we practise a ministry of healing in its widest possible sense.

My friend is a vicar. We trained together at St John's College, Nottingham, and as well as having a brilliant sense of humour, he is a really deep and engaging thinker. He also has cerebral palsy. Naturally, he has thought a lot about healing and has been prayed for by a lot of different people to be healed. But what if he doesn't need to be healed so much as the people around him need healing in order to see him as a full and valued member of the community, with all the gifts and abilities that he has to offer, just like anyone else? What if God needs to heal my 'ableist' prejudices, rather than any sort of deficiency in him? I was fascinated when I first heard of his sense of what the new creation will mean for him. He expects to have cerebral palsy, because that has always been a part of who he is, and to suddenly not have it would be to take on an identity that is alien to him. It has been through that wound that he has known both life and the God of all life.

Now this is certainly not to say that I do not believe in healing, physical or otherwise. I do. But it is to question what we mean by healing and perhaps to call us to exercise just a little more humility and grace in some of the situations that we might minister into. I sometimes hear it said that we shouldn't pray 'your will be done' when we pray for the specifics of healing, because we already know what God's will is. I'm not so sure. Who could ever have guessed that the way to healing in its fullest sense lay in a Messiah being crucified? Who expected those wounds to be there on Jesus even after his resurrection? '"For my thoughts are not your thoughts, neither are your ways my ways", declares the Lord' (Isaiah 55:8). If it was good enough for Jesus, in the garden of Gethsemane, to admit to the Father what he would choose to happen, and yet then to surrender himself to the Father's wisdom—'yet not my own will, but yours'—then I wonder why it isn't good enough for me. Surely true healing isn't dependent on the forcefulness of my prayer, nor the cognitive certainty of what I think will happen, but instead the loving goodness of our Father in heaven?

In this, perhaps we need to be reminded of what Martin Luther said about prayer: 'Prayer is not overcoming God's reluctance. It is laying hold of his willingness.'[24] Your kingdom come, your will be done, on earth, as in heaven.

The fact that Jesus still bears the wounds of the cross speaks to me in another way as well. Sometimes we live through the most painful experiences: the death of a loved one, a traumatic incident of some form, the pain of being let down by someone that we had trusted. Healing can certainly come—usually over time, but sometimes perhaps more quickly—through prayer, through the support of others, and in all those things through the grace of God. The memory of that thing doesn't go away from us: in this sense, the wound of it is always with us. And yet, because of the resurrection, our wounds can be redeemed. For Jesus, his scars no longer spoke of the despair of suffering and crucifixion but of the glory of resurrection and new life. They were transformed from a testimony of what the enemy had sought to inflict, to become a witness of all that God had overcome. And so it can be for us: by stepping into the power and hope of Christ's resurrection, our wounds no longer testify so much to our pain, as to the grace and power of God made complete in our weakness (2 Corinthians 12:9). In this way, it may be that our greatest ministry will stem from our deepest wounds. As one hymn writer put it: 'Those wounds, yet visible above, in beauty glorified.'[25]

As with the emphasis on the 'first day of the week', the repetition of 'peace be with you' (v. 21) stresses its vital importance.

Then Jesus commissions his disciples with the words, 'As the Father has sent me, so I send you.' One of the biggest theological moves of the 20th century was from seeing mission as an aspect of the church, to seeing it as an aspect of God himself. 'It is not the church of God that has a mission in the world, but the God of mission who has a church in the world,' Tim Dearborn reminds us.[26] Thus, the disciples of Jesus, both then and now, are called to continue the mission of God that was brought to a climax in the work of Jesus Christ. As Tom Wright has said, if new creation is a piece of music, then in Christ, God has written it, and our job is now to perform it. Christ has accomplished the defeat of sin and death. Our job is to live out this new reality in the world. In our own strength this would be an impossibility. But then God has not asked us to do it in our own strength.

Thus, Jesus breathed on them and said, 'Receive the Holy Spirit' (v. 22). The parallel again with Genesis is clear. In

Genesis 3:8, 'They heard the sound of the Lord God walking in the garden at the time of the evening breeze.' Now on the evening of the first day of new creation, a different wind blows through the room. And just as in Genesis 2:7, 'the Lord God formed man from the dust of the ground and breathed into his nostrils the breath of life, and the man became a living being', so now Jesus breathes on them the Holy Spirit, the breath of life, the breath of new creation. (See the poem 'Pentecost' at the end of this book.)

It is interesting to note how John's account of the giving of the Spirit differs from that of Luke–Acts.[27] For Luke, Calvary and Pentecost are separate events, with 40 days in between; for John, however, the crucifixion/resurrection and the giving of the Spirit are much closer together. Tracking how this can work out in practice can be very worthwhile. Some Christians have clearly been influenced more by the Luke–Acts account, and have ended up with a 'cross-stage' of the work of God in forgiveness and a 'Spirit-stage' of the power that he gives. However, the danger with disconnecting the two is that the work and ministry of the Spirit can become separated from the work of the crucifixion, and we can end up talking about power in ways that are very un-crosslike. The focus *can* become an overly triumphalistic message—of power, victory, breakthrough, and the like—with very little recognition of the reality of suffering and pain. In Martin Luther's terms, sometimes we can be in danger of wanting a 'theology of glory' apart from a 'theology of the cross'.

Perhaps the account of the giving of the Spirit in the Gospel of John is one that we need to draw on more fully, together with that from Luke–Acts. In John, Jesus' wounds remain; the risen Christ is still the crucified Christ. For John, cross and Spirit are not separate stages; the way of the cross and the way of the Spirit are one and the same. Thus, 'The Spirit leads us, as he led Jesus, to glory fashioned in suffering, to a victory won through defeat, to power exercised in weakness, to a throne that is the same shape as the cross.'[28]

Of course, the primary purpose of being filled with the Holy Spirit is for the church to announce, and to pronounce, the forgiveness of God (v. 23)—the peace with God, the *shalom*—that comes through sins forgiven, which is the gift of the cross. As part of this, there is the task to 'retain sins'—to remind people, in a sinless society, of the mess, the muddle, and the entanglement that sin always brings in its wake.

Contemporary disciples and a 'proper confidence'

In modern Western society, like the first disciples in the upper room, we can be afraid. We are afraid, in fact, of so many things. But not least afraid of telling other people about Jesus.

A recent *Church Times* survey[29] revealed that only one-quarter of Anglicans who responded were in the habit of inviting people to church. (In spite of this, 40 per cent of Anglicans believed that their church would grow over the next twelve months, even though recent figures suggested that only 18 per cent of Church of England churches are, in fact, growing. Quite how those in the first group thought that their churches might grow without a corresponding culture of invitation and welcome is an interesting question to ponder!) However, if there is such reluctance to invite people to church, what chance is there for those same people to be willing to share their faith themselves, especially in the current religious climate? A *Daily Telegraph*

ICM survey in 2014 revealed that 62 per cent of practising Christians felt that Christians in the UK are afraid to express their beliefs because of the rise of religious fundamentalism.

In such a climate, there is much to draw from the life and writing of Lesslie Newbigin, not least in his thoughts on Christians having a 'proper confidence' in the gospel. In the 1930s, Newbigin went to South India as a missionary and then, for 27 years, served as a bishop in the newly formed ecumenical Church of South India. When he returned to England in the 1970s, he taught and wrote extensively on mission. His sense was of a country that had become essentially secular and pagan: 'England is a pagan society and the development of a truly missionary encounter with this very tough form of paganism is the greatest intellectual and practical task facing the Church.'[30]

There can be little doubt that things have only continued on that trajectory since then. By 2012, the Church of England was attracting just under 800,000 worshippers to its churches on a typical Sunday, less than half the levels of the 1960s. However, there remain complexities in the societal picture, as 56 per cent regard Britain as a Christian country, a figure which rises to 73 per cent among the over 65s. Lord Williams, formerly Archbishop of Canterbury and now master of Magdalene College, Cambridge, was asked, 'Is Britain still a Christian country?'

If I say that this is a post-Christian nation, that doesn't mean necessarily non-Christian. It means the cultural memory is still quite strongly Christian. And in some ways, the cultural presence is still quite strongly Christian. But it is post-Christian in the sense that habitual practice for most of the population is not taken for granted... A Christian nation can sound like

a nation of committed believers, and we are not that. Equally,
we are not a nation of dedicated secularists. I think we're a
lot less secular than the most optimistic members of the British
Humanist Association would think.[31]

In such a climate, there are perhaps two equal but opposite dangers that Christians can fall into in regard to sharing the 'good news'. The first is that of arrogance. Perhaps recently, this has been most typified by members of Westboro Baptist Church, an American unaffiliated Baptist church known for its extreme ideologies, especially against gay people. Although small in number, the church has gained a disproportionate perception in the public eye through mass media coverage of their frequent protests and picketing of various events, usually with a 'God hates...' type of message. No doubt there are other Christians who, while not on the scale of Westboro, might also be described as 'arrogant' in their refusal to listen, wishing only to speak; their sense of having 'neat theologies' perfectly sown up in every area and ready to impose on others whether they like it or not; their message of threat and aggression, rather than of grace and invitation.

Yet on the other hand there is the danger of timidity. When Lesslie Newbigin returned from India, he was struck by the fear of Christians in England:

As time went on I began to receive invitations to take part in
conferences... I began to feel very uncomfortable with much that
I heard. There seemed to be so much timidity in commending
the gospel to the unconverted people of Britain.[32]

In a postmodern society, there can be a reluctance to challenge the relativism of the age with the message that there is a unique claim made by Jesus Christ. And in a society where religious fundamentalism is so prevalent, there can be the fear that to make any claims that might look in any way 'exclusive' would risk being lumped together with the likes of Westboro in the public imagination. In such a climate, Newbigin emphasises the importance of the church owning a 'proper confidence' in the unique revelation of God in Jesus Christ and the ability of the gospel of Jesus Christ to speak into, and transform, contemporary society. This goes beyond the narrow, brittle confidence of fundamentalism and stands in contrast to the clear lack of confidence shown in reductionist liberalism.

Jon Kuhrt helpfully draws out two aspects of Newbigin's thinking that help us to have more of a proper confidence within our context.[33]

Firstly, the gospel is public truth. The Christian claim cannot be relegated to some supposedly private sphere but exists as a confession of faith made squarely in the public domain. The central gospel message, that Jesus Christ is Lord, is not and has never been, about the formation of a private spiritual club—no one would have persecuted the early Christians, nor indeed would they Christians today, for that! The option of being yet another society that offered personal salvation was available, but clearly rejected in that the church was recognised as a movement launched into the *public* life of humankind. Hence, as Paul and his companions proclaimed the good news of Jesus, they were accused of acting in defiance of the decrees of Caesar by saying that there is another king, namely Jesus (Acts 17:7), Seen properly, the gospel is a declaration that calls all other would-be powers to submit:

Therefore God also highly exalted him
and gave him the name
that is above every name,
so that at the name of Jesus
every knee should bend,
in heaven and on earth and under the earth,
and every tongue should confess
that Jesus Christ is Lord,
to the glory of God the Father. (Philippians 2:9–11)

Thus, in spite of the culture of fear that exists for proclaiming and witnessing to the good news of Jesus, there simply is no option to escape the world and turn to a privatised expression of faith, in order to appease an increasingly secularised society.

However, the claim that the gospel is public truth does potentially leave the church open to the claim of arrogance mentioned above. This is certainly the case when it comes to an examination of how the church as an institution has sometimes dealt with the power at its disposal; obvious examples include the Crusades and tolerance of the slave trade, in certain places, for many centuries, though there are countless further examples where power has been used in order to oppress. In such situations, confidence in the gospel has been twinned with a failure to be honest about the failings of the church. If public confession of faith is needed, then public confession of human failing in the church is also required. There is no option to sidestep questions of power.

Power at its most basic level is influence, which Christians should surely seek in all spheres for the good of the kingdom. Thus, a use of power modelled on the servant-kingship of Jesus is imperative. Jesus washed the disciples' feet, 'knowing that the Father had given all things into his hands, and that he had come from God and was going to God' (John 13:3, NRSV). Similarly, the church's proclamation of Jesus as Lord must lead it to serve community and society, and not lord it over them.

In fact, this already happens in a number of different ways. A quarter of regular churchgoers across the denominations are involved in voluntary community service outside the church—a significantly higher proportion than for non-churchgoers. Churchgoers overall contribute 23.2 million hours of voluntary service each month in their local communities outside the church. Furthermore, Church of England congregations give more than £51.7 million each year to other charities—that's even more than the BBC's annual Children in Need appeal. There is definitely a task to be carried out in making the wider public more aware of the significant good done in society in the name of Jesus Christ, and to continue doing it.

So, for Newbigin, it is imperative to recognise the gospel as public truth.

Secondly, the biblical doctrine of 'election', or the calling of God's people, needs to be properly understood. There is undoubtedly a tension in the Bible between the universality of God's love for all people, and the particularity or uniqueness of his revelation through Jesus Christ. All too often this has been misunderstood as meaning that God calls one particular group of people (Israel/the church), to the exclusion of the rest. However, Newbigin argues that 'the key to the relation between the universal and the particular is God's way of election—the doctrine that permeates and controls the whole Bible. The one (or few) is chosen for the sake of the many; the particular is chosen for the sake of the universal.'[34]

Thus, when God chooses Abraham (Genesis 12)—and through Abraham, the people of Israel—it is not that God is blessing one group of people to the exclusion of the rest of the world. Rather, God is blessing one group of people that *through* them his blessing might flow out to the rest of the world. 'I will make you into a great nation, and I will bless you. I will make your name great, and you will be a blessing… and all peoples on earth will be blessed through you' (12:2–3). The particular is blessed for the sake of the universal. In the same way, even when Israel is disobedient and taken into exile, God's plan according to Isaiah 49:6 is to bring about a restoration; yet not for their sake alone, but that they might be 'a light to the nations, that my salvation may reach to the end of the earth'. In the same way, the church is not to be smug in a sense that it has been called while the rest of the world is damned; no, the church is called, not to hold on to the blessing of God that it has received, but rather to let that blessing flow out of it, far and wide.

All too often the church has got lost in discussions about the *scope* of election ('who's in and who's out') rather than the *purpose* of election—to declare and display God's saving power for the sake of the whole world. In the words of Jon Kuhrt:

> *The misunderstanding of the nature of election has been a disaster in missionary theology because so often those elected have considered themselves the sole beneficiaries of God's blessing rather than those charged with the message to share and to live out. We have focussed on future reward rather than our current responsibility. This has led to fruitless speculation about 'who gets to heaven' rather than the task of bearing witness to God's forgiveness and saving love now.*[35]

I have been fortunate to make two trips to the Holy Land. There are two seas in Israel—the Sea of Galilee and the Dead Sea. The Sea of Galilee is alive: it is still fished by local people and its banks are alive with lush vegetation. In stark contrast to the Sea of Galilee is the Dead Sea. It is appropriately named, because nothing lives in its waters. The land that surrounds it is barren and desolate. Both seas are fed by the same water supply, the River Jordan. What accounts for the one being alive and the other dead? The answer is simple: the Sea of Galilee not only receives fresh water from the Jordan, but it gives that same fresh water on to the Dead Sea. However, while the Dead Sea receives the fresh waters from the Jordan, it has no outlet; it doesn't give, it hoards all that it receives, and is thus dead. In the economy of God, the particular always exists for the sake of the universal; we are always blessed that we might be a blessing to others.

In summary, then, the gospel is unavoidably public truth, and the blessings that stem from it exist for the sake of the whole world.

Moving from 'fear' to 'confidence' as his disciples

There can be no doubt that the change in the first disciples of Jesus Christ was astonishing: from a group of people locked inside a room through fear, they became men and women who shared boldly the good news of Jesus, irrespective of opposition, arrest, persecution and death. How can we possibly explain such a change? By at least two factors: first, they encountered the risen Christ and saw his wounds; second, they were filled with the Holy Spirit.

In encountering the risen Christ and seeing his wounds, the disciples came to realise that death had no hold on Jesus.

And, since they too were in Christ, it could have no hold on them. What greater threat can people make than to threaten to take your life? But if you know that the grave has already been overcome, its power defeated, then you are free. And what a freedom they lived with. I mentioned in the opening chapter how, according to church tradition, the overwhelming majority of the first disciples were martyred. Having seen the risen Christ, they stopped holding on to their lives, knowing that, even if they were to lose them, they would gain resurrection. So often we define 'passion' today based on the rush of feelings we may have about something; in fact, 'passion', stemming from the cross of Christ, is about what you are willing to die for.

A modern-day example of a disciple who lived his life in such freedom and abandon is Jim Elliot. On 8 January 1956, he was killed while on a mission to an unreached tribe in Ecuador. He was only 28 years old. To many, this seemed like a huge waste of a life—one taken well before his time. Yet Elliot's own journal entry from just over six years earlier (28 October 1949) revealed an altogether different perspective; Elliot was living in the greatest freedom one could ever imagine. In the entry for that day, he wrote: 'He is no fool who gives what he cannot keep, to gain what he cannot lose.'

Encountering the risen Christ and seeing his wounds freed the first disciples from fear. Then they were filled with the Holy Spirit. The same power that raised Jesus Christ from the dead is alive in those who call themselves his disciples today. As Paul writes to the church of Ephesus:

I also pray that you will understand the incredible greatness of God's power for us who believe him. This is the same mighty power that raised Christ from the dead and seated him in the

place of honour at God's right hand in the heavenly realms.
(Ephesians 1:19–20, NLT)

The disciples were ordinary people, but what was bringing them to life was extraordinary. And the result was that they were empowered in extraordinary ways to live out their ordinary lives as witnesses to the risen Christ. As Michael Green has written:

They went everywhere spreading the good news which had brought joy, release and a new life to themselves. This must often have been not formal preaching, but the informal chattering to friends and chance acquaintances, in homes and wine shops, on walks, and around market stalls. They went everywhere gossiping the gospel; they did it naturally, enthusiastically, and with the conviction of those who are not paid to say that sort of thing. Consequently, they were taken seriously, and the movement spread, notably among the lower classes.[36]

Celsus, the second-century Greek philosopher and opponent of early Christianity, testified that 'Christians won converts not through public debate among elites but through quiet witness in their homes and places of work.'[37] Thus, witness in the early years of the church was not centred on professional evangelists or big-budget church programming, but, rather, low-profile relational approaches that all of us are capable of in the ordinary and the everyday.

A similar proposal was made in a radical report of the Church of England Commission on Evangelism entitled 'Towards the Conversion of England', published in 1945, immediately after World War II. One of its conclusions was:

The clergy are far too few to do more than touch the fringe of the problem of evangelising the whole country. It is only possible for the Gospel to reach the whole population through the active cooperation of all church people. We are convinced that England will never be converted until the laity use the opportunities for evangelism daily afforded by their various professions, crafts and occupations.

Seventy years on, this remains, if anything, even more true. As the numbers of clergy and paid church leaders decline, it is all the more urgent that the whole church plays its part in sharing the good news of Jesus Christ, in all the networks of relationships that we find ourselves in. It was always the intention that every Christian would be a witness to the resurrection. Each of us must be ready, gently and respectfully, to give an account for the hope that is in us (1 Peter 3:15). If we were put on the spot and asked tomorrow why we are a Christian, could we answer that? If we were asked to articulate the good news of Jesus, could we do that? We prepare properly for so many other aspects of our lives; we must ensure that we are properly prepared to speak of the most important news of all.[38]

Conclusion

For us modern-day disciples, there are two futures open to the church. In the words of the late David Watson, we can either 'evangelise' or 'fossilise'. The latter will be the path initially taken by disciples united by fear and kept inside the four walls of a building together. However, things need not be this way. That which brought about decisive transformation in the lives of the first disciples can do the same for us today. The modern-day church needs to encounter the risen Christ afresh, to see his wounds, and to know that, in him, nothing has a hold over us but the power of his all-conquering love. We need not be afraid, either to save our faces or hold on to our lives, 'for whoever wants to save their life will lose it, but whoever loses their life for me and for the gospel will save it' (Mark 8:35). Second, we need to ask afresh for Jesus to breathe the breath of the Holy Spirit upon us—for only in this peace and in this power will we be able to go. 'As the Father has sent me, so I am sending you' (John 20:21).

We need a 'proper confidence' in the gospel of Jesus Christ, just as the apostle Paul wrote: 'For I am not ashamed of the gospel, because it is the power of God that brings salvation to everyone who believes: first to the Jew, then to the Gentile' (Romans 1:16). And we need the courage to speak it out, and live it out, again like Paul who asked of the Ephesian Christians: 'Pray also for me, that whenever I speak, words may be given me so that I will fearlessly make known the mystery of the gospel, for which I am an ambassador in chains. Pray that I may declare it fearlessly, as I should' (Ephesians 6:19–20).

Finally, there is always a danger that our perspective on church growth and decline can become far too gloomy and inward-looking. To counter this we need a bigger vision on this issue, which can only come by seeing ourselves as part of a global Church.[39] As we look at the bigger picture, there are many encouraging conclusions to inspire us. For example, the church is still growing in Europe and North America, even if the increase is small. Molly Wall, the programme director of Operation World, notes that 'evangelical Christianity grew in strength and confidence in most European countries from the 1990s to the present, even while the overall population grew slowly or even declined'.[40] Even more encouragingly, the church has seen dramatic growth in Asia, Africa and

South America, with particularly explosive growth in the African church.

It can surely only be a residual colonial mindset in Western Christianity that would want to play down such exciting moves of God in places like this. Christians in Nigeria and South Sudan are facing extreme levels of persecution and yet the church is still growing. What could we learn from our brothers and sisters in these places as we increasingly take up a position of witnessing from the margins of our own culture? Are we 'teachable' enough to listen? Putting all the statistics together shows that Christianity is comfortably the world's largest religion with more than 2.4 billion Christians worldwide, covering just over one-third of the world's population. Meanwhile, atheism is in global decline. Often the perspective that we carry, based on our parochial bubbles or from the media, is simply incorrect. We are part of a global Church and that global Church is growing! And even if our piece of that global big picture is in decline, we can still draw comfort from the words of G.K. Chesterton: 'Christianity has died many times and risen again, for it had a God who knew the way out of the grave.'[41] There are reasons aplenty for the church in our day to minister out of a proper confidence.

Pause and reflect: 'The Fellowship of the Unashamed'

The following is a piece of prose. There appears to be uncertainty over its origin, but whatever its source, it speaks of someone who has encountered the risen Christ and been filled with the power of the Holy Spirit. Here is someone who knows a confidence in the good news of Jesus, and has the courage to proclaim it:

I'm part of the fellowship of the unashamed. I have the Holy Spirit power. The die has been cast. I have stepped over the line. The decision has been made. I'm a disciple of His. I won't look back, let up, slow down, back away, or be still.

My past is redeemed, my present makes sense, my future is secure. I'm finished and done with low living, sight walking, smooth knees, colourless dreams, tamed visions, worldly talking, cheap giving and dwarfed goals.

I no longer need pre-eminence, prosperity, position, promotions, plaudits or popularity. I don't have to be right, first, tops, recognised, praised, regarded or rewarded. I now live by faith, lean on His presence, walk by patience, am uplifted by prayer and I labour with power.

My face is set, my gait is fast, my goal is heaven, my road is narrow, my way is rough, my companions are few, my Guide is reliable, my mission is clear. I cannot be bought, compromised, detoured, lured away, turned back, deluded or delayed. I will not flinch in the face of sacrifice, hesitate in the presence of the enemy, pander at the pool of popularity or meander in the maze of mediocrity.

I won't give up, shut up, let up, until I have stayed up, stored up, prayed up, paid up, preached up for the cause of Christ. I am a disciple of Jesus. I must go until He comes, give until I drop, preach until all know and work until He stops me. And, when He comes for His own, He will have no problem recognising me. My banner will be clear!

Discussion questions

- What does 'fear' look/sound/taste/feel/smell like? How would you describe it?
- What do you make of the differences between the way that John narrates the giving of the Holy Spirit and the account found in Luke–Acts? Have you ever noticed this difference before?
- Do you agree that Christians today are afraid of sharing their faith? If so, why do you think this is?
- Do you agree that the gospel is 'public truth', and with the understanding of 'election' given here? What difference could these things make in practice?
- Have you ever known a 'proper confidence' in sharing the good news of Jesus? Have you ever seen it in someone else?

Chapter 4

Thomas: Doubt and Confirmation

Immediately the boy's father exclaimed, 'I do believe; help me overcome my unbelief!' (Mark 9:24)

Anything worth believing is also worth doubting.[42]

A defendant was on trial for murder. There was strong evidence indicating guilt, but no corpse. In the defence's closing statement the lawyer, knowing that his client would probably be convicted, resorted to a trick: 'Ladies and gentlemen of the jury, I have a surprise for you all,' he said as he looked at his watch. 'Within one minute, the person presumed dead in this case will walk into this courtroom.'

He looked toward the courtroom door. The jurors, somewhat stunned, looked on eagerly. A minute passed. Nothing happened. Finally the lawyer said, 'Actually, I made up the previous statement. But you all looked on with anticipation. I therefore put it to you that there is reasonable doubt in this case as to whether anyone was killed and insist that you return a verdict of not guilty.'

The jury, clearly confused, retired to deliberate. A few minutes later, the jury returned and pronounced a verdict of guilty. 'But how?' enquired the lawyer. 'You must have had some doubt; I saw all of you stare at the door.'

The jury foreman replied, 'Oh, we looked, but your client didn't!'

Doubt, or the lack of it, can be very revealing. It certainly was in the case of Thomas.

'Doubting' Thomas

If, among the twelve that Jesus chose, there had been a 'worst disciple' competition, church history has judged that second prize should have gone to Thomas. He is one of the disciples who is well known for all the wrong reasons. In fact, it is almost impossible today to think of him without prefixing the word 'doubting' to his name.

Aside from his encounter with the risen Christ, there is only fleeting mention of Thomas in the Gospel stories. We know that he is called as a disciple (Matthew 10:3; Mark 3:18; Luke 6:15), but in the Synoptic Gospels this is all that we are told of him. John offers but two vignettes that give us the briefest of glimpses into his character and personality.

In the first episode (John 11:1–16), Jesus receives word that his close friend Lazarus has died and, following a delay of a couple of days, decides to go to Bethany in order to raise him to life. The disciples, however, are well aware of the dangers that this may involve, given that the Jews there recently tried to stone Jesus. Their reluctance is perhaps understandable, though Jesus is determined that they should visit. Thomas then speaks to the group of disciples: 'Let us go too so that we may die with Jesus.' Maybe this was spoken with all the passion and enthusiasm of the gloomy donkey Eeyore from A.A. Milne's Winnie-the-Pooh stories. Or perhaps, above all the other disciples, he understood what it really meant to follow Jesus.

In the second episode (John 14:1–6), Jesus is preparing his disciples for his departure and trying to reassure them that they should not be worried about the future. He tells them that he is going to prepare a place for them in which there is plenty of room for all, and that they all know the place to which he is going. They are soothing words, leading to deep and profound trust. Except that Thomas is having none of it! He jumps straight in to point out that, in actual fact, Jesus is quite wrong since they *don't* know where he is going, so how on earth can they know how to get there? Honest and direct, he is asking the sort of question a child would ask but an adult might be afraid to, for fear of embarrassment. But Thomas isn't embarrassed and just comes out with it.

Thomas, then, is a figure who doesn't always 'get' things the first time, but is unafraid to question and to challenge. We're not always great at dealing with characters like him in the church. Fortunately, Jesus' grace and patience show us a different way.

Thomas *doesn't* encounter the risen Christ

Now, as it turns out, Thomas wasn't present with the disciples when they encountered the risen Christ—locked in the room as they were, full of fear. Quite where Thomas was, though, is anyone's guess. Did he have other, more pressing commitments? Was he ill? Did he forget about the new meeting time? Whatever the reason, he wasn't there. He didn't see, hear, or experience all that they had done in that life-changing encounter the previous week, when they discovered that Jesus really was alive. Even worse, they now wanted to tell him *all* about it. It must have felt a bit like sitting through that endless photo slideshow with your friend who tells you that such-and-such-an-event was 'just AMAAAZING!' and that 'you really should have been there!'

When Mary reported to the disciples that she had seen the Lord, there was no indication that any of them doubted what she said. But when all the other disciples report the same thing to Thomas, not for the first time, he is having none of it. Not one to accept things at face value, or at the first time of asking, he says, 'Unless I see the nail marks in his hands and put my finger where the nails were, and put my hand into his side, I will not believe' (John 20:25). For these immortal words, Thomas has earned his place in history as 'Doubting Thomas'—the second worst disciple of the twelve.

What a week must have then followed for Thomas! Like us, the disciples were far from a perfect bunch, but no doubt they had a sense of solidarity about them; a sense of having lived together through some extraordinary times over the past few years; a recognition of having shared communally some of the most powerful, confusing, incredible experiences together. But suddenly Thomas isn't a part of that. He is detached from the group. They are together, but he is isolated. Did he genuinely not trust their account, or did he secretly wish that he had been there last week, just in case they were telling the truth? Did he really not believe or was he just begrudging the fact that he himself hadn't been a part of it? To have followed in vain a failed Messiah must have been hard enough; it cannot have been easy now to have this glimmer of (false?) hope, relayed to him second-hand, and causing him to become detached from those he had shared his life with for several years. Thomas has been looked down on throughout church history, but I confess that I have some sympathy with him.

Thomas *does* encounter the risen Christ

Now Thomas (also known as Didymus), one of the Twelve, was not with the disciples when Jesus came. So the other disciples told him, 'We have seen the Lord!'

But he said to them, 'Unless I see the nail marks in his hands and put my finger where the nails were, and put my hand into his side, I will not believe.'

A week later his disciples were in the house again, and Thomas was with them. Though the doors were locked, Jesus came and stood among them and said, 'Peace be with you!' Then he said to Thomas, 'Put your finger here; see my hands. Reach out your hand and put it into my side. Stop doubting and believe.'

Thomas said to him, 'My Lord and my God!'

Then Jesus told him, 'Because you have seen me, you have believed; blessed are those who have not seen and yet have believed.' (John 20:24–29)

A week later, the disciples are in the same place again. The early Christians didn't stop going to the synagogue or the temple, but in addition to this they met in each other's houses. Sunday quickly became the day for such gatherings—not the Saturday of the sabbath, but the Sunday of Easter; the day of resurrection and new creation.

This time Thomas *was* with them. Obviously his diary was clear, or he had recovered from that illness, or he'd remembered what time he needed to turn up. The important thing is that he was there. Interestingly, though, as with the previous week, the doors were again locked. Hadn't they encountered the risen Christ? Hadn't he spoken words of peace to them? And hadn't he breathed the Holy Spirit on them? Well, yes. But very often change—genuine transformation—takes more than just a single event. As much as we sometimes wish that we could click our fingers and be 'different', there is a road of transformation that we must walk—a process of being remoulded and remade that we must submit to. Very often, genuine, lasting change simply takes time.

So the disciples are there, as are Thomas and—very soon, too, in spite of the locked doors—Jesus. What is remarkable, though, is the grace and kindness of Jesus in meeting Thomas exactly in the place of his doubts. Thomas' doubts are not condemned or judged. He is simply invited, beckoned, to see the evidence for himself—to put his fingers into Jesus' hands and his hand into Jesus' side—then to move on from his doubts to embrace a new faith in the resurrected Saviour who stands before him. As we can see from paintings such as Caravaggio's *The Incredulity of Saint Thomas*, it may be that Thomas really did need the physical contact with Jesus in order to believe.[43] However, I like to imagine that the sight of Jesus alone, in front of him, was enough to provoke the response 'My Lord and my God!' Though invited to touch Jesus, this was no longer necessary for Thomas to believe. According to Jesus, though, God's blessing rests on those people who neither touch nor even see the physically resurrected Jesus, and yet, in faith apart from the senses, still believe—people like us, today.

The benefit of the doubt

What cannot be denied about the story of Thomas encountering the risen Christ is the way that it reveals to us what Greg Boyd has termed 'the benefit of the doubt'.[44] Perhaps it was the entire possibility of the resurrection for one person in the midst of history—not stored up for all the faithful at the end of history—that troubled Thomas. Or perhaps Thomas realised more quickly than the other disciples what the resurrection would mean about who Jesus was, and needed time to wrestle with this. Either way we should not miss the fact that the disciple who doubted Jesus the most gives the highest evaluation of him uttered in any gospel—that he is divine.

And yet at times in the church today, doubt in its broadest sense can so often be viewed with suspicion. There are perhaps at least three possible reasons for this.

The first is the issue of power in the church. Many Christians can feel, or be made to feel, guilty for expressing doubts or questions, lest they be seen to question the authority of the teaching of the church or their leader, the reliability of scripture, or the cohesiveness of Christian theology. So they keep quiet, pushing the doubts away and hoping they stay away. Second, the cultural context of modernity has promoted a view of knowledge in which precise, certain, factual knowledge has reigned supreme. As the church has fought hard to express faith within such a context, there perhaps hasn't been as much room for ambiguity, uncertainty and doubt as there should. And third, sometimes it's easier just to be told the 'answers' by the 'experts' and not to face the difficult option of thinking for oneself and wrestling with difficult issues. I mean, life is hard enough; at least in church, we can escape all of that and embrace a 'simple faith', can't we? Many commentators have observed that the church can sometimes be like a swimming pool in which most of the noise comes from the shallow end.

In response to this, we should note three further points.

First, *doubt is biblical*; there is such a thing as 'faithful doubt'. The heroes of faith throughout the pages of scripture were not static, unwavering pillars who went through their lives not questioning the things of God—quite the opposite! Think, perhaps most obviously, of Job. With Job's life turned upside down, he refuses to respond with pious speech but accuses God of acting ruthlessly. Job's so-called friends rush in to justify God. When God finally appears on the scene, it is to say that neither Job nor his friends understand what they are talking about. But while Job is commended for speaking right, laying out his doubts honestly, his friends are rebuked severely. Or think of the psalms. Around 40 per cent of these are lament, or complaint, psalms—laying out doubts and problems to God in no uncertain terms, sometimes holding God as personally responsible, even negligent in the situation. All but one of these psalms arrive at praise in the end, but only after expressing negative emotions openly.

In the New Testament, think of John the Doubter. Now we know him as John the Baptist, but, looking at Matthew 11:2–11 in isolation, the story could have been so different. John is in prison, having been arrested by Herod, and sends word to his disciples to ask Jesus: 'Are you the one who is to come, or are we to wait for another?' Who had devoted his life to preparing Israel for the coming of the Messiah? John. Who had introduced Jesus to the public? John. Who had said Jesus was so great that he wasn't worthy even to tie his sandal? John. Who had baptised him? Who had heard the voice from heaven affirming Jesus as God's Son? Who had seen the Holy Spirit descending upon him as a dove? John. Who had pointed to Jesus and proclaimed, 'Behold! The Lamb of God who takes away the sins of the world'? John. Yet here he is, in prison, doubting, and needing reassurance. And what is the response of Jesus? To condemn John? No, Jesus affirms him and answers his question.

Then, of course, there is Jesus himself. In Gethsemane, he clearly wrestles in agony as to what is the right path ahead; praying that the cup of suffering, his forthcoming crucifixion, be taken from him. Jesus did not know with certainty what the right course of events was, but he surrendered and 'was obedient to death, even death on a cross' (Philippians 2:8). He committed himself to follow the Father's way, even when that came at huge cost to himself. And then on the cross the following afternoon, he cries out, 'My God, my God, why have you forsaken me?' It's a cry of dereliction: 'God, where are you?' It was doubt expressed in the words of one of the psalms already mentioned, but also unflinching commitment to walk the Father's way.

The Bible, therefore, demonstrates that there is such a thing as 'faithful doubting'.

Second, *doubt is beneficial*. As one T-shirt slogan has it, 'Age is just a number; maturity is a choice.' It is not possible to grow in maturity without working through doubts and questions about faith. There are lots of 'stages of faith' models out there, but I'm drawn to the stripped-down version by Brian McLaren, which sees people moving through four stages: simplicity, complexity, perplexity, and harmony/humility.[45] Churches sometimes seem to keep people at the level of simplicity in terms of their faith, even while they are handling multiple complexities at home or work. They are adults in the rest of their lives but when they step into church they are in effect treated as children. Complexity, though painful and something we often seek to avoid, is an essential part of growing up. And doubt can strengthen faith. As Brad Watson has said, in relation to his book *Raised? Finding Jesus by Doubting the Resurrection*, 'Anything worth believing is also worth doubting.'

When we arrived in Ripon, my son was a Liverpool FC fan—just like his dad, and just like his dad's dad. However, as he tried to fit in with his new peers, his confidence in the side began to waver. He began to talk about following Real Madrid, Barcelona and even Manchester City! For a time, I wanted to force his hand regarding his allegiance; however, I knew that I couldn't do this. So I gave him the space to 'doubt' and to think things through for himself. Interestingly, over time, he came to own his allegiance to the club for himself and became more passionate than he had been before his doubts. (So much so, that my concern now is about idolatry, rather than doubt!) He's a bit like Thomas, perhaps—the disciple who was the biggest doubter but who also offered the highest recognition of who Jesus was.

Third, it needs to be recognised that we have often embraced a *wrong understanding of faith*. In the words of Mike Yaconelli, 'Faith has been reduced to a comfortable system of *beliefs* about God instead of an *un*comfortable encounter with God.'[46] 'Faith' has become the psychological certainty of what we think about God, rather than our relational commitment to God. In this, importance has come to rest on our intellectual convictions about particular beliefs and doctrines, which in some parts of the church cannot be questioned, wrestled with or doubted. Similarly, to pray effectively for someone or something is seen as being mentally convinced that the outcome we request will happen.

However, God desires a genuine relationship with his people, not a tick-box assent to particular beliefs or a slot-machine approach to prayer. Interestingly, the word for 'faith' in New Testament Greek can mean both 'faith' and 'faithfulness'. We need to recapture faith as relational, coven-antal commitment—faithfulness: he is our God and we are his people. It's a relationship for the long haul—a marathon, not a sprint.

In September 2013, I entered the 2014 London Marathon,

pledging to raise more than £2000 for Cancer Research in memory of my dad. Was I certain then that I would be able to finish the race? Was I certain that I would raise the required amount of money? On both accounts, no. I wasn't certain but I was committed. In spite of plenty of doubts on both scores, I persisted with both my training and my fundraising. On dark and wet evenings, I went out running even when I didn't feel like it. I badgered people to sponsor even when I felt awkward about it. And on 13 April 2014, I finished the race with little strength to spare but having raised over twice as much as I needed to. The certainty wasn't always there but the commitment was.

Doubting the resurrection

'Anything worth believing is also worth doubting.' Given the central importance of the resurrection of Jesus Christ to the Christian faith, it is well worth the individual Christian taking time to explore the evidence that surrounds the resurrection of Jesus Christ. The atheist Richard Dawkins has said, 'If the Resurrection is not true, Christianity becomes null and void.'[47] Ironically, Paul said something remarkably similar, though from a somewhat different angle: 'And if Christ has not been raised, your faith is futile' (1 Corinthians 15:17).

1 Peter 3:15 says, 'But in your hearts revere Christ as Lord. Always be prepared to give an answer to everyone who asks you to give the reason for the hope that you have. But do this with gentleness and respect.' Apologetics (from the Greek *apologia*, 'speaking in defence') is the discipline of defending a position (often religious) through the systematic use of information. It is something that Christians have been doing from the earliest years of the church.

Logically, the apologetics that surround the resurrection presuppose an apologetic case having already been made for the existence of a historical Jesus. There is much that could be said on this, but I will leave *The Times* columnist Matthew Parris, himself an 'avowed atheist', to make the case:

Did Jesus of Nazareth ever really exist?... Look for the elements that don't really fit. They are the least likely to have been made up. In the Church's 2,000-year history, the character and teachings of Jesus are the bits that don't fit. There is an annoying knot of gristle at the very centre of the Christian Church, and it is called Christ. Chew and chew though Christians do, time and again pushing this indigestible, discomfiting and in some ways unlovely object to the edge of the ecclesiastical plate, they cannot obliterate it. It is not least for this that I, an avowed atheist, feel such huge respect for him. If Jesus Christ had not existed, it would most certainly not have been necessary for the Church to invent someone like him.[48]

I am convinced by the logic of Parris' case.

However, moving on to the case for, or against, the resurrection itself, anyone wishing to explore its credibility would have to address at least three central purported facts that surround it: first, the discovery of an empty tomb by a group of female followers on the Sunday morning after the crucifixion; second, a number of 'resurrection appearances' reported by various individuals and groups, including those described in these chapters; and third, the origin of the early Christians' belief that God had raised Jesus from the dead.[49]

First, it stands to reason that the tomb of Jesus, owned by a member of the Jewish Sanhedrin named Joseph of Arimathea, was empty when the disciples began to preach that Jesus was raised from the dead. To have done so when the tomb was occupied would have been ridiculous; besides, if that were indeed the case, opponents would have quickly pointed out the obvious problem. It is interesting that no dispute seems to have taken place over the remains of any corpse purported to be that of Jesus. The Jewish claim in Matthew 28:11–15 was that the body had been stolen, which presupposes the fact of an empty tomb. Some critics have felt compelled to argue not only against the empty tomb of Jesus, but also against his burial in the way described in the Gospels. However, as John A.T. Robinson observes, the burial of Jesus in the tomb is 'one of the earliest and best-attested facts about Jesus'.[50]

This burial is reported in extremely early sources, such as the Passion Story, which many think underlies Mark's writing of the suffering and death of Jesus, as well as the old Christian tradition that Paul passed on to the Corinthian church in 1 Corinthians 15:3–5. Furthermore, the fact that Joseph of Arimathea was noted as a member of the Jewish Sanhedrin seems an incredibly unlikely detail were it not true. This concurs with Matthew Parris' comment above: 'look for the elements that don't really fit'. Yet even more surprising, indeed embarrassing, is the claim that it was female witnesses who first saw the empty tomb. Given the low place of women on the social spectrum and the fact that they were not regarded as credible witnesses, this claim that they were the first witnesses to the resurrection of Christ and the empty tomb would only make sense were it true. Any fantasy or legend would undoubtedly have chosen male witnesses to shore up its spurious claims—not so the Gospels!

Second, there is the evidence that a number of individuals and groups saw the resurrected Jesus. Early Christian tradition—not included in the Gospels—claimed that Peter had seen the risen Christ. Paul vouches for this in 1 Corinthians 15:3–8, while it is also mentioned in another old Christian tradition found in Luke 24:34. Furthermore, the other disciples had seen him too—Paul again confirms this to the Corinthians, while there are other accounts in the Gospels in John 20:19–20 and Luke 24:36–43. These are, in fact, the best attested resurrection appearances of Jesus. Furthermore, Paul refers to 500 witnesses seeing the risen Christ simultaneously. This is an extraordinary claim and, though not mentioned in the Gospels, can only have been cited by Paul if he had known at least some of the people involved—hence his pointing out that most of them were still alive.

Paul mentions an appearance to 'all the apostles' (1 Corinthians 15:7), which must be a wider group than the Twelve (who are mentioned separately in verse 5). Again, this only makes sense if Paul had personal contact with them. There is, of course, the appearance to Paul himself, which we came across in the Introduction. Such a change in the orientation of his life, together with the costliness of it to him personally, would only be credible if he had truly encountered the risen Christ himself. However, perhaps the most intriguing appearance is that to Jesus' younger brother, James. It seems that James, together with the rest of the family, did not believe in Jesus in any way during his lifetime (compare Mark 3:21, 31–35; John 7:1–10). Again, by the criteria of embarrassing evidence, this can only make sense if it is true. The fact that Jesus' brothers, not least James, come to find their place among the early Christian believers (Acts 1:14), with James as one of the pillars of the church in Jerusalem (Galatians 2:9) and eventually its sole head (Acts 21:18), only makes sense if Jesus was resurrected and encountered by James and his brothers. Crucifixion alone would only confirm the sense of delusional pretensions that they thought Jesus had carried during his lifetime.

Third, there is the question of why the Christian faith sprang into origin midway through the first century AD. Again, Jews had no concept in any way of a Messiah who would be executed in shame and defeat as a common criminal. This expectation did not fit any of the available moulds for a Messiah. Yet Christians from the earliest times claimed that this was exactly what had happened to Jesus of Nazareth and they still held to their belief that he was Israel's true Messiah. Such a belief can only be possible if they based their surprising and unexpected claim on the reality of Jesus' resurrection from the dead. Resurrection was meant to happen to the whole nation of Israel at the end of time. Instead, they claimed that it had happened to one person—Jesus Christ—in the middle of time. Again, such a claim, which broke apart their worldview, can only be explained if it were actually what they had seen and experienced with their own senses. Furthermore, as we have seen, almost all the early Christians gave their lives for the sake of the risen Christ. What sense would this make if they knew they were only faking or deluding people into believing in the resurrection?

These three facts—the empty tomb, the resurrection appearances, and the origins of Christianity—must be explained by any theory that seeks to make sense of what happened on that first Easter weekend. Of course, many different theories have been put forward. For example, there are the claims that the disciples stole the body; that Jesus was never really dead in the first place; that his body was moved by Joseph of Arimathea without the disciples knowing; that the so-called 'appearances' were, in fact, only hallucinations.

Yet each of these, for me, fails to do justice to the three central facts that we have explored.

The first fails, among other things, on the grounds that it supposes that the disciples were expecting the resurrection of Jesus and hence needed to fake it in some way. As we have seen, resurrection within history was simply not contemplated in the first century. The second fails on the same grounds, as well as ignoring the fact that the Romans were experts at execution and would have known when a criminal was dead or not—hence, the purpose of the sword in the side (John 19:34). The third, while being implausible in itself, has nothing to say at all, either on the resurrection appearances or on the origins of the Christian movement. Finally, the hallucination hypothesis explains neither the empty tomb nor the rise of Christianity. Furthermore, it does not make sense of the quantity and scale of the resurrection appearances: one person may experience a hallucination but not such large groups as were claimed by Paul and in such separate contexts. Besides, such visions would only serve to convince people that the person they saw was really dead—not that they were now alive again!

The only theory that, to my mind, makes sense of all the evidence satisfactorily is that Jesus was bodily raised from the dead. Only this can explain the awkwardness of the empty tomb, which was not denied by the Jewish authorities; the embarrassment of the female witness to the resurrection; and the surprising rise of the early Christian movement. However, like Thomas, we may need to explore this for ourselves before fully believing. Remember: 'Anything worth believing is also worth doubting.'

The challenge of the resurrection is not just about getting our thoughts or words or arguments right, but getting our lives right as well. The greatest apologetic to a watching world is for the church to practise a lifestyle of resurrection—the power of love, grace, forgiveness and holiness. On the other hand, as Brennan Manning observes, 'The greatest single cause of atheism in the world today is Christians who acknowledge Jesus with their lips and walk out the door and deny Him by their lifestyle. That is what an unbelieving world simply finds unbelievable.'[51]

For this reason, the writer and speaker Pete Rollins was once asked whether he denied the resurrection, to which he answered:

> *Without equivocation or hesitation I fully and completely admit that I deny the resurrection of Christ. This is something that anyone who knows me could tell you, and I am not afraid to say it publicly, no matter what some people may think…*
>
> *I deny the resurrection of Christ every time I do not serve at the feet of the oppressed, each day that I turn my back on the poor; I deny the resurrection of Christ when I close my ears to the cries of the downtrodden and lend my support to an unjust and corrupt system.*
>
> *However there are moments when I affirm that resurrection, few and far between as they are. I affirm it when I stand up for those who are forced to live on their knees, when I speak for those who have had their tongues torn out, when I cry for those who have no more tears left to shed.*[52]

The challenge of Thomas

Thomas has gone down in history as the second worst disciple of Jesus. But is there another angle on him? Mike Yaconelli certainly thinks so:

Thomas, one of Jesus' disciples, is probably best known for his curiosity. Thomas believed in Jesus, trusted him, followed him, was willing to die for him, but he was infected with a risky curiosity. When everyone else said they had seen Jesus after the Crucifixion, Thomas wasn't satisfied. He wanted more. He wanted to touch Jesus, hear Jesus, see Jesus, embrace Jesus. Most theologians have labelled Thomas a 'doubter'. 'Doubting Thomas' is the negative spin they have labelled to Thomas's questioning. I disagree. Thomas wasn't doubting Jesus, he was longing for Jesus. Curiosity is a hunger of the soul, and because Thomas was strong and courageous and spoke bluntly, he was daring enough to ask tough questions. He was not refusing to believe, he was refusing to settle for secondhand faith. Thomas was driven to know the truth—to mingle with it, wrestle with it, become intimate with it. Jesus didn't criticise Thomas for his questions. He honoured his curiosity. Jesus legitimised Thomas's holy curiosity. Childlike faith looks a lot like the faith of Thomas—daring, reckless, bold, and aggressive.[53]

Maybe Thomas was refusing to settle for second-hand faith because he wanted a first-hand encounter. Perhaps we need to be challenged by Thomas' example, rather than simply dismissing it. Where are we not engaging with the tough questions of life and faith? Where are we settling for simplicity rather than journeying through the complexity? Where are we too passive—happy to live off other people's experiences, settling for their second-hand encounters—rather than hungering for a passionate encounter with the risen Christ for ourselves?

C.S. Lewis described Aslan, the Christ figure in 'The Chronicles of Narnia', as 'not a tame lion'.[54] It surely follows that there should be something 'untamed' about those who came after the untamed Christ. Yet so much of the church today has been tamed. In the words of Mike Yaconelli again:

> *Our world is populated with domesticated grown-ups who would rather settle for safe, predictable answers instead of wild, unpredictable mystery. Faith has been reduced to a comfortable system of beliefs about God instead of an uncomfortable encounter with God.*[55]

We looked in the last chapter at a group of tamed disciples who learned to become untamed again, as they encountered the risen Christ and the life of the Holy Spirit was breathed upon them. That same encounter and that same life-giving power are available to us today, if only we would dare to receive them.

Like Thomas, once we have encountered the risen Christ, let us go and tell others about him. The other disciples were still in the same place, the upper room, a week later—they had been sent, but they don't appear to have gone (just yet)! However, tradition records that Thomas was the first of the disciples to leave Jerusalem. Whatever doubt and scepticism he may have had, he made a theological leap that not one of the others did: 'My Lord and my God.' Once he was sent, he didn't waste any time going. And he went further than all the other disciples—reputedly all the way to the tip of India, where he would give his life for Jesus as a martyr. If that is how far Thomas went with his 'doubt', then we could all do with some. Was he the second-worst disciple? I don't think so.

Pause and reflect: A Franciscan benediction

May God bless you with discomfort
at easy answers, half-truths
and superficial relationships,
so that you may live
deep within your heart.

May God bless you with anger
at injustice, oppression
and exploitation of people,
so that you may work for
justice, freedom and peace.

May God bless you with tears
to shed for those who suffer pain,
rejection, hunger and war,
so that you may reach out your hand
to comfort them and
to turn their pain to joy.

And may God bless you
with enough foolishness
to believe that you can
make a difference in the world,
so that you can do
what others claim cannot be done
to bring justice and kindness
to all our children and the poor.
Amen.[56]

Discussion questions

- How did you view Thomas before reading this chapter? How has your view of him changed by the end of it?
- Do you agree or disagree with Mike Yaconelli's depiction of Thomas? Can you explain why?
- Do you agree that there is a 'benefit of the doubt'? Are there any other benefits not given here? What are the downsides of doubt?
- Have you ever had doubts in your journey of faith so far? How did you/might you go about addressing them?
- Do you agree that 'so much of the church today has been tamed'. Can you explain why or why not?

– Chapter 5 –

Cleopas (+1): Shattered Dreams and New Beginnings

Forget the former things; do not dwell on the past. See, I am doing a new thing! Now it springs up; do you not perceive it? (Isaiah 43:18–19a)

We offer everything to God except our hopes and dreams. (Michael Thompson)[57]

'Dreams. Dreams. Dreams. Wake up!' So said Bill Cosby to the class of 2012 at Temple University's 125th commencement. 'You've got plenty of time, but don't dream through it. Wake up!' Dreaming can sometimes be a means of escaping present reality; of displacing the effort of an all-too-ordinary existence, for the ease of a future in which the dream has already 'all come true'. Dreaming can also be a painfully narcissistic exercise, wherein 'my dreams' are the centre around which the rest of the cosmos is expected to orbit.

The context for this chapter, though, is a different sort of dreaming—a dreaming that is rooted in the kingdom of God and seeks after the doing of God's will in the world. Yet, sometimes, even these dreams do not come off. So what do we do when such dreams come crashing down around us? How do we go on when the things that we thought were of God don't work out? This is akin to what Cleopas and his companion must have been thinking as they journeyed from Jerusalem to Emmaus. Many of us will have had similar experiences in our own lives.

All the encounters in this book so far have come from the Gospel of John, but this encounter comes from the Gospel of Luke. In Luke, rather than lots of post-resurrection encounter stories, there is a particularly famous one, before Jesus meets the disciples as a group. More commonly, it is called the 'road to Emmaus' story. At the level of drama, it has everything: there is sorrow, suspense, confusion, slow realisation before sudden astonished recognition, and then joyful exuberance at the end.

To recognise as fully as possible the drama of this story, we will explore it in sections.

The two companions

Now that same day two of them were going to a village called Emmaus, about seven miles from Jerusalem. They were talking with each other about everything that had happened. (Luke 24:13–14)

The story begins with two companions on the road together, journeying about seven miles from Jerusalem to a village called Emmaus. We are given the name of one of them as Cleopas in verse 18. Very probably this is the same person as 'Clopas', whose wife Mary appears among the women at the cross in John's Gospel.[58] However, no matter who they were, they were journeying this road together. The word 'companion' comes from the Latin words for 'bread' (*panis*) and 'together' (*com*). Cleopas and Mary (we will assume she is the unnamed person for sake of ease) are, therefore, those who, figuratively but later literally too, eat bread together. The image is of people on a journey who mutually sustain, feed and nourish one another. Do we have people like this in our lives?

The (un)known stranger

As they talked and discussed these things with each other, Jesus
himself came up and walked along with them; but they were
kept from recognising him. He asked them, 'What are you
discussing together as you walk along?' (Luke 24:15–17a)

As Cleopas and Mary are making their way along the road,
Jesus comes alongside them, but they are unable to recognise
him. As we have seen above, this is a very common feature of
the post-resurrection stories. The risen Christ *is* present, but
the issue is always our recognition of, and attentiveness to,
his presence there with us. And this stranger-Jesus asks them
a question. As Conrad Gempf demonstrates in his excellent
book *Jesus Asked*, 'nothing was more characteristic of Jesus'
speaking than the fact that he constantly asked questions'.[59]
This was not about him wanting to find out something that he
didn't already know, but rather him wanting to know where
people were in their relationship to him. These questions
were not about wanting to know facts, but wanting to know
people. Thus, they were asked, 'What are you discussing with
each other while you walk along?'—a question that brought
their journey to a temporary halt, as a deep sadness came
across their faces.

The shattered dream

They stood still, their faces downcast. One of them, named
Cleopas, asked him, 'Are you the only one visiting Jerusalem
who does not know the things that have happened there in these
days?'
'What things?' he asked.
'About Jesus of Nazareth,' they replied. 'He was a prophet,

powerful in word and deed before God and all the people. The chief priests and our rulers handed him over to be sentenced to death, and they crucified him; but we had hoped that he was the one who was going to redeem Israel. And what is more, it is the third day since all this took place. In addition, some of our women amazed us. They went to the tomb early this morning but didn't find his body. They came and told us that they had seen a vision of angels, who said he was alive. Then some of our companions went to the tomb and found it just as the women had said, but they did not see Jesus. (Luke 24:17b–24)

The reason for their grief is made clear. They, together with so many, had regarded Jesus not only as a prophet but as the one who would 'redeem' Israel. To speak of redemption was to invoke the metaphor of the slave market, in which someone with the money would pay a price in order to take slaves under his ownership. However, the metaphor had particular resonance for Israel in the defining story of its exodus from slavery in Egypt. The hope had been that what God had done all those years ago, in leading his people to freedom through the waters of the Red Sea, he would do so once again. Having liberated them once from pagan domination at the hands of the Egyptians, he would do again, this time from the Romans. In fact, Luke has already taken up this very metaphor in his account of the transfiguration, and specifically the topic of conversation between Jesus, Moses and Elijah—namely, his own departure or 'exodus' (Luke 9:30–31). The reference is very deliberate and very loaded.

No wonder, then, that his crucifixion was such a shock. He was meant to be doing all the defeating, not getting defeated himself. And yet, of course, being crucified was precisely how Jesus *was* redeeming Israel. These, then, were two complementary rather than antagonistic ideas. This was only true, however, because of the event that changed everything—the resurrection of Jesus Christ—and Cleopas and Mary had not quite caught up with the risen Christ as yet. They were still living in the darkness of confusion: they had heard reports from the women of an empty tomb and of angels announcing that he was alive. Others had confirmed the state of the tomb but had not themselves seen Jesus alive. Mary and Cleopas were not yet able to make sense of all that was happening around them.

The Scriptures explained: 'burning hearts'

He said to them, 'How foolish you are, and how slow to believe all that the prophets have spoken! Did not the Messiah have to suffer these things and then enter his glory?' And beginning with Moses and all the Prophets, he explained to them what was said in all the Scriptures concerning himself. (Luke 24:25–27)

As Jesus makes clear, the problem of the disciples is that they have been reading the story of the Bible all wrong. 'And beginning with Moses and all the Prophets, he explained to them what was said in all the scriptures concerning himself.' How fascinating it would have been to hear exactly the words that Jesus used to do this. Yet what is abundantly clear is that, whatever exact words he used, they were not just a few isolated 'proof' texts but rather a telling of the whole story of what we call the Old Testament, to show how it had come to a climax in the events of those past three days.

As Tom Wright explains, the problem of the disciples was akin to that of looking through the wrong end of a telescope and seeing everything in the wrong perspective.[60] They had seen the story as being how God would redeem Israel *from* suffering, when, in fact, it would be the story of how he would redeem Israel *through* suffering—not least the suffering of Israel's representative, her King or Messiah, namely, Jesus himself. No wonder, then, that Cleopas and Mary would later reflect on how their hearts were burning as they heard Jesus expound the story of the scriptures!

The meal shared: 'opened eyes'

As they approached the village to which they were going, Jesus continued on as if he were going further. But they urged him strongly, 'Stay with us, for it is nearly evening; the day is almost over.' So he went in to stay with them.

When he was at the table with them, he took bread, gave thanks, broke it and began to give it to them. Then their eyes were opened and they recognised him, and he disappeared from their sight. (Luke 24:28–31)

As they draw near to Emmaus, Jesus keeps walking as if he is going somewhere else; but after being strongly urged, comes in to stay with them and to eat. Eating is such a significant thing throughout the Bible, and what is about to unfold will resonate with the very first meal in the scriptures, that of Adam and Eve:

*When the woman saw that the fruit of the tree was good for food and pleasing to the eye, and also desirable for gaining wisdom, she took some and ate it. She also gave some to her husband, who was with her, and he ate it. **Then the eyes of both of them were opened** [my emphasis], and they realised they were naked. (Genesis 3:6–7)*

That was a moment of death and decay coming upon creation, as the eyes of Adam and Eve were opened to the reality of their sin and rebellion. Now, Luke is describing the first meal of the new creation. As Jesus takes the bread, gives thanks to God, breaks it and gives it to them, 'their eyes were opened, and they recognised him'. Again, eyes are opened—no longer to sin and rebellion, to death and decay, but now to their hitherto unrealised encounter with the one who, by his death and resurrection, has created the world anew, full of life, joy and new possibility. And just as the penny drops, Jesus vanishes from their sight—a reminder that the risen Christ is always a little more elusive than we would like him to be; we are always playing catch-up with him.

The new beginning

They asked each other, 'Were not our hearts burning within us while he talked with us on the road and opened the Scriptures to us?'

They got up and returned at once to Jerusalem. There they found the Eleven and those with them, assembled together and saying, 'It is true! The Lord has risen and has appeared to Simon.' Then the two told what had happened on the way, and how Jesus was recognised by them when he broke the bread. (Luke 24:32–35)

Having been caught up in this spiritual whirlwind, they decide to go straight back to Jerusalem. As we have seen, once we have truly encountered the risen Christ, we feel compelled to make him known to others—not through any dead sense of obligation or duty, but through the vibrant imperative of *having* to share with others the radical, transforming difference that he has made to our lives. As Cleopas and Mary meet their wider companions, and hear their testimony of Jesus being alive and having appeared to Peter, so their own testimony is able to confirm this in the way that they themselves encountered Jesus on the road and in the breaking of the bread.

This is a reminder of the power of bearing witness to the living reality of the risen Jesus in our lives. The disciples started by sharing their testimony of having encountered the risen Christ with one another in Jerusalem, but then they were called to take the message of Jesus' death and resurrection, and the call to turn from sin and receive forgiveness, out from Jerusalem to the ends of the earth. They are to be witnesses of these things (vv. 46–48). Perhaps it is only when we can confidently and regularly share our own stories of the living God at work in our lives with other believers that we will be able to bear witness to him among those who do not yet know him or who have turned away from him.

Our shattered dreams

The dream

Have you ever had any dreams that didn't come to be? Things you thought were of God but came crashing down around you?

My wife, Sarah, and I met at university in York. We were young and hopelessly naive, but had a similar passion for God, and similar dreams of how we might give ourselves to serve him. We got married in the summer of 2000 and faced the immediate decision of where we might live and what we might do. In a sense, we could go anywhere: we had no ties or responsibilities at that time. Young and carefree, there was a real sense of openness about the future that lay in front of us. We thought, we prayed, we considered the options.

The most important person in the formation of my faith during the previous difficult teenage years was my youth leader. It wasn't always so much what he said that inspired me, but the love and hospitality, humility and generosity, fire and passion, that he modelled in the way he lived. Together with his wife and children, he modelled to me—and to many others in our youth group—a living, breathing replica of what Paul had sought to model to the Thessalonian Christians: 'So deeply do we care for you that we are determined to share with you not only the gospel of God but also our own selves, because you have become very dear to us' (1 Thessalonians 2:8, NRSV).

As Sarah and I considered our options, there was one that, while not the most glamorous, just wouldn't go away. My friend who had been my youth leader was part of the leadership team of a house church in Leeds, and was being prepared by the person who had originally planted that church to take on the overall leadership within a year or so. He was inviting Sarah and me to move to Leeds and be a part of his dream to lead a church that would be a little bit different. There would be less 'churchiness' and more of what really mattered—passionately worshipping and seeking God, and urgently reaching out to the community around us. His vision inspired and captured us; we wanted to be a part of it. I would take a lead with the musical worship in the church, Sarah with the youth and schools work.

In the early days, the dream was so very exciting, as we helped to lead and shape a small but growing church community. We started to glimpse the potential that exists when a group of people truly believe that God can empower and use them to reach the people and community around them. The opportunity to do this with friends and companions seemed even more of a gift, and very soon two of our other friends from my teenage years came to be a part of things in Leeds too. They were people we knew, loved and had journeyed with for years. What an opportunity it was to be part of something really exciting for God! What could possibly go wrong?

The dream shatters

As time went on, problems began to emerge. It is sometimes hard to keep a dream in tension with the ordinary reality that is daily life. Why does change so often seem so slow? Why do the signs of God's coming kingdom not come more fully? Full-time jobs—mine was as a secondary school teacher—sometimes felt like an obstacle in the way of what we really wanted to be doing. A pioneering leader can find it hard when change doesn't come quickly enough, or when a vision is shared and yet some in the church cannot quite grasp it. For a wider leadership team, the challenge is how much you are there to support the main leader, and how much to represent the rest of the church. And what happens when the two begin to grow apart and you find yourselves caught in the middle? As these tensions began to emerge, so did our sense of being relatively young, naive and inexperienced in leadership; of feeling increasingly exposed and out of our depth.

The stress and pressure of the situation exposed the weaknesses of all our personalities: aggressive moves and defensive responses; overeager desires to bring matters to a head, and vain hopes that problems could simply be brushed under the carpet. There were faults on all sides, both in things said and done, and in things not said and not done. The problem of a lack of wider accountability, that we had never seen as something of great importance, suddenly seemed a glaring omission.

Eventually, the leader stepped down and left the church. Sarah and I tried to stay, but things were never the same again. The dream had very much died, and we were living on in the aftermath. I was done with church leadership. In fact, had it not been for the fact of having children, I probably wouldn't have wanted even to be part of a church for a while. As it was, we sought temporary refuge in a church big enough for us to feel anonymous for a time, yet with enough people that we already knew there. Having gone part-time as a teacher to run a gap-year discipleship programme for a few years, I was back teaching at the same school full-time again. But something kept nagging away at me that this wasn't where I was meant to be for ever. I couldn't escape the feeling that to do what I really wanted to do—teaching people about Jesus, shaping them in faith and discipleship, equipping them for mission—I needed to be exercising leadership in the church.

We had been burned, however, and I felt reluctant to give myself to such work again. When dreams go wrong, is it possible to dream again? Whether in words or in actions, there are some who clearly believe 'no': it's too dangerous, too risky to open yourselves up to hurt again. Dreaming, like any form of loving, makes you vulnerable. But what sort of life is it not to love, not to dream? Must we from now on only seek to aim low for fear of being disappointed again? I have come to believe that it is possible to dream again; but that it cannot be the same as before. Following the 'stages of faith' model outlined in the previous chapter, our initial 'simplicity' in moving to Leeds had been hit by 'complexity' and 'perplexity'. But the option to return to 'simplicity' wasn't there. The only option was whether to stay in confusion, and possibly bitterness, or to journey on to a new place of 'harmony' and 'humility'.

A new beginning

The French philosopher Paul Ricoeur pointed towards the possibility of a 'second naivety'. The innocence of the 'first naivety' for us was gone for ever. But I believe that it is possible to 'go again' with a renewed passion for God, albeit a more considered passion, which is more aware and informed of the realities and complexities that exist in the world around us. 'Beyond the desert of criticism we wish to be called again,' wrote Ricoeur.[61] That is to say, even after having faced the difficult questions, there is still the opportunity to step out afresh in faith.

For myself, I found I was caught in a pincer movement to explore my sense of vocation again, as I talked with the chaplain at the school where I was teaching, as well as the clergy at the church where we were now worshippers. Both were part of the Church of England, and, against my non-denominational upbringing and house church experience, it felt, to my surprise, that this was where God was leading me. I couldn't say anything with certainty; maybe eight years before, I would have been able to do so. But my sense of certainty in aspects like this had died with all that had gone wrong. The process of discerning vocation to ordained ministry in the Church of England, then, was a real gift to me. It allowed me to explore things, and for others to discern prayerfully as well, without everything resting on my personal sense of certainty.

Events took their course and I was accepted to train at St John's Nottingham for three years. From there, I went to serve my curacy at Holy Trinity Ripon. I do not know for certain where my ministry will take me, but I have found a way of dreaming again of what God can do through me. The first naivety may have died, but I have found a second naivety that I treasure even more in its place. In spite of old dreams being shattered, I know that the risen Christ always wants to lead us into new beginnings.

Persistence and resilience in our dreaming

The other day I listened again to Martin Luther King's famous 'I have a dream' speech, delivered on 28 August 1963 to over 250,000 civil rights supporters from the steps of the Lincoln Memorial during the march on Washington. The speech called for an end to racism in the United States and was a defining moment in the American Civil Rights Movement. As I listened to it, I was struck afresh by both the persistence and the resilience of King's dreaming.

King's dreaming was *persistent*. 'There are those who are asking the devotees of civil rights, "When will you be satisfied?"' he said, before going on to detail the plight of black people in the United States. Police brutality, discrimination in public places, lack of social mobility, segregation, and the denial of the vote were all things which led King to conclude: 'No, no, we are not satisfied, and we will not be satisfied until justice rolls down like waters and righteousness like a mighty stream.' He knew what the goal was and he had an unsatisfied persistence until the people of America got there.

As part of this persistence, King's dreaming was also

resilient. Throughout the civil rights campaign, King was the target for arrests, constant anonymous death threats, and a night-bombing of his home. Bitter efforts were made to break the campaign through all kinds of harassment, abuse and persecution. Yet, through it all, he was resilient enough to keep persisting towards the goal of a just and equal America.

> *I am not unmindful that some of you have come here out of great trials and tribulations. Some of you have come fresh from narrow jail cells. Some of you have come from areas where your quest for freedom left you battered by the storms of persecution and staggered by the winds of police brutality. You have been the veterans of creative suffering. Continue to work with the faith that unearned suffering is redemptive.*

His response, in spite of all of this: 'I say to you today, my friends, so even though we face the difficulties of today and tomorrow, I still have a dream. It is a dream deeply rooted in the American dream.'

Thus it must be for all who would keep dreaming for God and for the coming of his kingdom, on earth as it is in heaven. Our dreams, too, must be persistent and resilient. Where is the evidence of our 'holy dissatisfaction'? Where are there situations in our world that simply should not be? Where is the belief in us that another world is possible? Between 1508 and 1512, under the patronage of Pope Julius II, Michelangelo painted the Sistine Chapel ceiling, a masterpiece without precedent that, arguably, was to change the course of Western art. Michelangelo was intimidated by the scale of the commission, and made it known from the outset of Julius II's approach that he would prefer to decline. However, he would later say: 'The greatest danger for most of us is not that our aim is too high and we miss it, but that it is too low and we reach it.'

So it is for many of us, not least when our hands have been burned and our dreams have been shattered. 'Once bitten, twice shy' becomes our mantra. 'Never again.' 'Aim low to avoid disappointment.' Regularly, we will need to allow God to keep reshaping the dreams that we have for him and his kingdom; to ensure that they remain his dreams and not solely ours. Sometimes, we will need to lay them down— for a season or, possibly, and no doubt painfully, altogether. But, with the God of resurrection, there will always be a new beginning.

Resources in dreaming for the kingdom

So where, through the setbacks and grind of life, have we stopped dreaming? Where do we need to encounter the risen Christ afresh in order to dare to dream once again? If we believe that God has given us a dream or a vision, we need to pray earnestly for the persistence and the resilience in order to hold on to it. In fact, we should ask God for a vision that is so big that, without him, it is impossible to fulfil.

To keep these dreams alive, to maintain both persistence and resilience, we will have to draw on the same elements as we found in the story at the heart of this chapter. First, we will need companions. It is hard to stress how important this is in contemporary discipleship. Perhaps it might be part of a marriage relationship, but the image of two (or more) people walking the same path together equally holds true outside marriage. Today we might call it all sorts of things: soul friends, prayer partners, accountability groups, as well as a host of other names. The point is that there is a close commitment to one another and a vital level of mutual support.

The sociologist Edward Hall divides our social world into four different spaces: public space, social space, personal space and intimate space.[62] The sense of a companion is very much concerned with the last of these—intimate space. The question for us all to ask ourselves is whether we have these sorts of people around us. It is very possible in the contemporary church to be among large groups of people, and yet never really experience an intimate depth of giving and receiving in a spiritual relationship. Yet, for me, cultivating those sorts of intentional relationships has been vital to my journeying deeper and further along the road of discipleship. We need people around us, of the same heart and the same mind, who will be able to strengthen us on our journey. Around such people we can explore what God might be saying to us, and doing in and through us at this time.

Secondly, and together with these people, we will need to encounter the risen Christ. In the road to Emmaus story, this happens in two ways: in hearing and meditating on the story of the scriptures, and in receiving the bread and wine of Communion. It is interesting how Bible reading is so often seen as an individual pursuit, as part of personal quiet times or daily devotionals, yet this was not always the case. For much of church history, the Bible was read overwhelmingly or even exclusively in community. We would certainly benefit today from recovering a more regular habit of reading the Bible with others. There are many ways to imagine this happening, the use of the Revised Common Lectionary being the most obvious,[63] allowing Christians across denominations to share a common Bible reading pattern. Equally, churches or small groups could take a common approach to reading the Bible for a season, allowing them to share insights and challenges whenever they gather together.

In a more contemporary sense, I have benefited from the (free) Bible in One Year app, produced by Nicky and Pippa Gumbel.[64] It has been particularly good to share on Twitter with other people across the country, and further afield, who are drawing inspiration from a particular day's reading.[65] The biggest Bible app is YouVersion[66] and this offers many different ways to interact with other people in reading the Bible. It is interesting to note how digital approaches to Bible reading are offering ways of reading more communally, socially and interactively.

Second, we need to draw strength from the bread and wine of Communion. Coming from a very 'low' church perspective, I have not always placed as much value on Holy Communion as I now do. As Robin Parry parodies it, 'McEucharist, the fast-food approach to Communion, was my world for many years.'[67] Part of the gift of the Church of England to me has been teaching me to take seriously both word *and* sacrament. Holy Communion captures the richness of the whole biblical story and acts out the fullness of the gospel; I love its physicality and the way it draws together all the senses; I draw strength from its remembering what Christ has done and anticipating all that is to come. In the words of Tom Wright, 'When [Jesus] wanted fully to explain what his forthcoming death was all about, he didn't give a theory. He didn't even give them a set of scriptural texts. He gave them a meal.'[68] As with all good meals, we come, not as individuals but as a community—as fellow companions on a journey together. All in Christ are welcome to come: there are no exclusions, for, in Christ, all barriers of separation, whether age or race or gender or social background, have been broken down (Galatians 3:28). I am always deeply moved, when giving out bread and wine, to see how the youngest hands and the oldest trembling hands all receive the same elements, drawing strength from them together.

In the Emmaus story, I believe Luke is drawing our attention to something powerful for Christians through the ages—that scripture and sacrament, the word and the meal, belong together: 'Therefore what God has joined together, let no one separate' (Mark 10:9). And yet, it is interesting that, as in so many areas, the easiest thing to do is to fly to one or other of the extremes. Generally speaking, those at the 'low' end of the church emphasise the word, while those at the 'high' end of the church emphasise the meal. Yet, in this story of burning hearts and opened eyes, it is through the powerful combination of both scripture and sacrament that the church is enabled to encounter the risen Christ most fully.

The incarnate word and the produce of grain and grape will 'earth' us in our dreaming for the kingdom, which is to come 'on earth as it is in heaven' (Matthew 6:10). They will fuel us to live in the ordinary and the mundane, the unhistoric areas of life, in which history is quietly being written and God is always to be found. In this way—contrary to Cosby's commencement speech, quoted at the beginning of this chapter—it is precisely *in* our dreaming for the kingdom that we find ourselves most awake. Maybe it's time to dream again?

Pause and reflect: 'Disturb us, Lord'

Disturb us, Lord, when
we are too well pleased with ourselves,
when our dreams have come true

because we have dreamed too little,
when we arrived safely
because we sailed too close to the shore.

Disturb us, Lord, when
with the abundance of things we possess
we have lost our thirst
for the waters of life;
having fallen in love with life,
we have ceased to dream of eternity;
and, in our efforts to build a new earth,
we have allowed our vision
of the new heaven to dim.

Disturb us, Lord, to dare more boldly,
to venture on wider seas
where storms will show your mastery;
where losing sight of land,
we shall find the stars.
We ask you to push back
the horizons of our hopes;
and to push into the future
in strength, courage, hope, and love.
Amen
ATTRIBUTED TO FRANCIS DRAKE

Discussion questions

- Which aspect of the road to Emmaus story grabs you the most? Why?
- Describe any shattered dreams that you have experienced.
- Who would you say your companions are/have been? What do they do for you on the journey of faith?

- How far do you think you get the right balance between scripture and sacrament? Has one ever been more important to you than the other? Have you noticed this change at all over time?
- What dreams do you have at the moment? How far would you describe yourself as persistent and resilient in your dreaming?

– Chapter 6 –

Peter: Failure and Restoration

For as high as the heavens are above the earth, so great is his love for those who fear him; as far as the east is from the west, so far has he removed our transgressions from us. (Psalm 103:11–12)

Failure is only the opportunity to more intelligently begin again. (Henry Ford)

I have a number of friends who are surgeons. I have noticed how much they delight in telling stories of their operations in far more detail than I would like. But I have also noticed that often in surgery, they have had to go deep in order to get to the root of what is causing the problem.

In this chapter we will look at a Bible passage in which we see Peter carrying deep, unhealed wounds. Those wounds stem from the powerful memories of a fateful night when he fell a long way short of what he had said he would do, and who he had aspired to be. Peter had promised Jesus at the Last Supper that he would be the most faithful of all the disciples—that even if all the others fell away under pressure, he, Peter, would remain steadfast to the end (Mark 14:29). Yet that very evening he denied Jesus three times.

He now faces the shame of not having lived up to what he hoped: the embarrassment of having let down one so close to him; the regret of knowing that, when the pressure was on, he failed, and failed badly. And Jesus, like a master surgeon, must gently expose and remove the shame that is the source of those wounds. Then he must clean up the mess that surrounds Peter, and so enable full healing to take place.

As we did in the last chapter, we will explore the drama of this passage in stages.

Scene 1: Fishing out at sea

Afterwards Jesus appeared again to his disciples, by the Sea of Galilee. It happened this way: Simon Peter, Thomas (also known as Didymus), Nathanael from Cana in Galilee, the sons of Zebedee, and two other disciples were together. 'I'm going out to fish,' Simon Peter told them, and they said, 'We'll go with you.' So they went out and got into the boat, but that night they caught nothing.

Early in the morning, Jesus stood on the shore, but the disciples did not realise that it was Jesus.

He called out to them, 'Friends, haven't you any fish?'

'No,' they answered.

He said, 'Throw your net on the right side of the boat and you will find some.' When they did, they were unable to haul the net in because of the large number of fish.

Then the disciple whom Jesus loved said to Peter, 'It is the Lord!' As soon as Simon Peter heard him say, 'It is the Lord,' he wrapped his outer garment round him (for he had taken it off) and jumped into the water. The other disciples followed in the boat, towing the net full of fish, for they were not far from shore, about a hundred metres. (John 21:1–8)

As so often in the Gospel stories, Peter takes the initiative ahead of the other disciples. Here he announces that he is going to go fishing and the other disciples say that they will go with him too. There is a great deal of speculation as to Peter's motives, but, given the flow of John's account, it seems that even though Peter had been to the empty tomb, and even though he had encountered the risen Christ as part of the wider group of the disciples, he would probably have believed that he himself had blown it as far as his relationship with Jesus was concerned. Risen or not risen was an irrelevance— Peter had failed Jesus and, whatever fresh adventures may have been in store for the disciples, there surely could not be a place for Peter as part of them. So Peter, along with six other disciples, went back to fishing.

Peter was returning to what he knew. After everything that had happened over the past few years—being called, against the odds, to follow Jesus, and being sent out to minister in ways he could never have imagined—it was now time to return to the life he was familiar with. It was time to leave behind his failure and go back to the security of that which he was confident he could do. After all the talk of 'fishing for people' (Mark 1:16–18), Peter went back to fishing for fish.

Except he couldn't catch any.

How infuriating this must have been for Peter! They were skilful fishermen, with years of experience in the trade, working in a place they knew like the back of their hands, in the ideal conditions of the night—and they couldn't catch a thing. Yet given the way John has been telling his story, perhaps we really shouldn't be surprised. After all, Jesus has earlier told his disciples, 'I am the vine; you are the branches. If you remain in me and I in you, you will bear much fruit; apart from me you can do nothing' (John 15:5). How often we skip over that last part. Yes, of course, we need Jesus for the really big stuff, but surely we're OK for the stuff that lies within our own comfort zones? Yet with this scene comes the reminder: apart from me you can do *nothing*. Not even catching a fish when you've been a fisherman all your life.

This must have been so demoralising for Peter. He had nothing of his own strength and ability to return to, nothing of himself on which to base his security, even after having failed so dramatically elsewhere. But Jesus is preparing Peter for their encounter that will follow, and, like Peter, we often need to be brought to the end of our own resources in order to encounter Jesus afresh.

Jesus stands on the beach, at daybreak—again hinting at the dawn of a new day that is breaking because of his resurrection. As with Mary at the tomb and the disciples on the road to Emmaus, he isn't recognised. Then this stranger tells the fishermen to cast their net to the right side of the boat, where they will find some fish. I can imagine how they might have reacted to that suggestion! Of course they'd already tried it, yet without Jesus it had failed. With Jesus, however, they suddenly catch so many fish that they can hardly haul the net in again. How are we to understand this? Surely the point isn't the success of a particular fishing technique; it's about the presence of a particular person—the risen Lord Jesus.

I wonder when we as Christians will learn the same lesson. At a time of concern about falling church numbers, it can be easy to shop around for fancy techniques and formulas in order to get things going again. So much of the Western church seems to be in search of the hidden formula, the magic bullet, the secret of success. A church experiencing growth somewhere else in the world is all too often taken as a sign that we, here, could grow too if only we used the same techniques. Of course, we must be prepared in humility to listen and learn from others. We must always remain teachable. But we surely must also be prepared to reflect prayerfully on issues of context and transferability; 'growth' is never simplistic and prepackaged in the ways that we are led to believe. If only we had the confidence to move past formulas and techniques and towards an encounter with Jesus himself.

Turning back to the story, we see that suddenly, with the great haul of fish, something clicks in Peter's memory. Jesus has deliberately taken him back, first of all, to that moment when Peter first encountered him (Luke 5:1–11). This is the first stage of Jesus' gentle healing surgery on Peter. On that night those few years ago, the disciples had been fishing for many hours; again, they had caught nothing, and a stranger had stood on the shore and told them to do something blindingly obvious—on that occasion, to put out into deeper waters and let down their nets. It was a different technique, but then, as we have seen, the technique was never the issue. What was important was that it was the same stranger. The same Jesus. The same outcome.

While it is the beloved disciple who now exhibits the quickest insight in identifying the stranger as Jesus, it is Peter, characteristically, who is quickest to action. Impetuous, spontaneous, spur-of-the-moment Peter hastily gets some clothes on and then jumps, without thinking, into the sea to reach Jesus. He has been denying his denials for too long. He knows that he has unfinished business with Jesus. He hopes against hope that there is still hope left for him. In doing so, he lets the other disciples do all the work of hauling in the net full of fish. But, like the decision of Mary to sit at Jesus' feet while Martha slaved away in the kitchen (Luke 10:38–42), there is again need of only one thing, and Peter has chosen the better part, which will not be taken away from him. With all that is in him, and with all the metaphorical baggage that he carries on his back through the water, he knows that the best place to be is with Jesus. The solution is not to run away from him, but to swim desperately towards him—to seek refuge in the one that he has failed so badly.

In Peter's position, would we do the same? What are we living in denial about? What hurts, guilt, or shame have we been suppressing? What failures are we hoping will go away, but they refuse to do so? Can we find the courage to rush towards Jesus, even in our failure and in our carrying of so much baggage?

Scene 2: Breakfast on the beach

When they landed, they saw a fire of burning coals there with fish on it, and some bread.

Jesus said to them, 'Bring some of the fish you have just caught.' So Simon Peter climbed back into the boat and dragged the net ashore. It was full of large fish, 153, but even with so many the net was not torn. Jesus said to them, 'Come and have breakfast.' None of the disciples dared ask him, 'Who are you?' They knew it was the Lord. Jesus came, took the bread and gave it to them, and did the same with the fish. This was now the third time Jesus appeared to his disciples after he was raised from the dead. (John 21:9–14)

Memory is a deeply multisensory thing. We can be taken back to past events through a sound that we hear again, an object that we see, the taste or texture of something, or maybe a smell. Each of these can act like a trigger mechanism that transports us back to a moment and a place in our memories—perhaps something that has been hidden away from our consciousness but which, through our senses, is rediscovered and brought afresh into the present moment. A smell as distinctive as a charcoal fire would do this. The second stage of Jesus' work on Peter has begun.

We read that 'when they landed, they saw a fire of burning coals' (v. 9), and for Peter, the smell would have instantly taken him back to that fateful night outside the high priest's house. On that occasion, the slaves and the attendants had made a charcoal fire, around which they were standing to warm themselves, and it was around this same fire that Peter came to stand, as Jesus was inside being interrogated (John 18:18). It was around this fire that Peter denied Jesus three times. So standing on the beach, dripping wet from a frantic swim, he must have suddenly felt nauseous, sick to his stomach, as his past confronted him right there in front of Jesus. I can't imagine he would have felt like eating anything for breakfast that morning.

Intriguingly, in spite of the great haul of fish that the disciples have caught, Jesus is already cooking fish on a fire. Teresa of Avila (1515–1582) once wrote that 'Christ has no body but yours, no hands, no feet on earth but yours.' While I appreciate the sentiment behind this saying, the danger of it, by itself, is that it might lead us to imagine that God is passive in the world, waiting for *us* to make things happen. I do not believe that he is. Yes, we are God's hands and feet in the places where we serve him; but God's action in the world is not limited to what *we* may or may not do for him. God is always at work in the world, and we are invited to collaborate with his mission and ministry within it. In this story, Jesus doesn't *need* Peter's fish, but he does invite him to bring it as a part of the meal.

In the same way, at the Communion table, as the church remembers the death and resurrection of Jesus Christ, it is Jesus again who has provided the meal. It is not about what we can do for him, but about what he has done for us. And it is only out of receiving first *from* him that we are then able to offer ourselves *to* him. St Augustine says:

You are the body of Christ. In you and through you the work of the incarnation must go forward. You are to be taken; you are to be blessed, broken, and given; that you may be the means of grace and the vehicles of the Eternal love. Behold what you are. Become what you receive.[69]

In this, the initiative is all God's; our role is to respond.

Returning to our story, we hear that 153 fish were brought on shore. The precise number of fish is a reference to Ezekiel 47:10 and the new life which is now at work in the world, making people children of God, because of the sacrificial death of Jesus.[70] In spite of this, and in contrast to the earlier account of a miraculous haul of fish (Luke 5:1–11), the net is not torn (v. 11). The resurrection of Jesus Christ has brought in a new world, and with it has opened up a whole new world of possibilities that could not have been conceived of before. Living within this world will require time for acclimatisation—hence the statement that 'none of the disciples dared ask him, "Who are you?" They knew it was the Lord.' This only makes sense if, again, the risen Jesus was similar to, but in some way different from, the way he was before. The future had arrived in the present ahead of its time: the disciples were like someone in the 16th century trying to make sense of seeing a person logging on to the internet.[71]

Scene 3: One-on-one with Jesus

When they had finished eating, Jesus said to Simon Peter, 'Simon son of John, do you love me more than these?'

'Yes, Lord,' he said, 'you know that I love you.'

Jesus said, 'Feed my lambs.'

Again Jesus said, 'Simon son of John, do you love me?'

He answered, 'Yes, Lord, you know that I love you.'

Jesus said, 'Take care of my sheep.'

The third time he said to him, 'Simon son of John, do you love me?'

Peter was hurt because Jesus asked him the third time, 'Do you love me?' He said, 'Lord, you know all things; you know that I love you.'

Jesus said, 'Feed my sheep. Very truly I tell you, when you were younger you dressed yourself and went where you wanted; but when you are old you will stretch out your hands, and someone else will dress you and lead you where you do not want to go.' Jesus said this to indicate the kind of death by which Peter would glorify God. Then he said to him, 'Follow me!' (John 21:15–19)

For me, this encounter between Jesus and Peter is perhaps the most tender, compassionate and transforming exchange in the whole Bible. Peter has been living with great shame; yet, in John's Gospel, Jesus is the Passover lamb who can take away the sins of the world—Peter's sin; my sin; your sin. This is the third and final stage of Jesus' work on Peter in which he forgives, heals and restores him.

Jesus addresses Peter as 'Simon son of John' (v. 15), taking Peter back again to the very beginning of his discipleship journey (John 1:40–42), before he was renamed Peter, with a new identity to fit a new vocation. Jesus first asks him, 'Do you love me more than these?' As for the identity of 'these', it perhaps makes most sense to read it as 'Do you love me more than these other disciples do?' Peter has always been the first to the action—claiming that he above all the others will follow to the end (Mark 14:29); being the first to draw his sword when people come to arrest Jesus (John 18:10).

Twice, Jesus asks Peter whether he loves him in the 'all-out' kind of way that Peter would always have claimed; twice, Peter replies with a more measured form of commitment. Finally, Jesus meets Peter where he is (as he always does with us), accepting the love that Peter offers, even though it doesn't match the strength of Jesus' own love for him. The three questions, of course, correspond to Peter's three denials. The hurt for Peter lies in his being taken back so vividly to that previous scene around the charcoal fire. Memory is not just a cognitive thing—instead, we experience our feelings again. For Peter, all of his shame is now flooding back.

Importantly, though, Jesus is bringing this shame to the surface, not in order that Peter might be condemned but in order that he might be healed. Jesus is finally rooting out the wound so as to bring about a full and complete restoration. Peter's pledge of a loving response to Jesus brings him to a place of humility—the humility of realising that he hasn't been able to be, or do, all that he hoped for. Yet, in this, he is also brought to a new place of security—the security of realising that love is no longer about what he can prove to Jesus through sheer impulsiveness, but is instead all about resting in Jesus' deep knowledge of him. As Peter's past shame is confronted, so, at the same time, his present commission is redefined. The call to 'feed my lambs', with its variants, invites Peter to share in the ministry of Jesus, the good shepherd (John 10:11). Ministry is first and foremost something that belongs to Jesus. Just as with the provision of food for breakfast on the beach, Jesus is not dependent on us; but, again, he does invite us to share his vocation with him.

Incredibly, in spite of all that has happened, Peter is to remain the rock on which Jesus will build his church. I wonder whether, today, we would ever give such responsibility to such an obvious failure. Jesus was willing to do so.

With his past shame confronted and his present commission redefined, Peter's future destiny is now revealed. For him, as for all the other disciples bar John, this will be a costly path to walk—that of martyrdom. According to church tradition, Peter was hung upside down on a cross, not considering himself worthy to suffer the same way up as Jesus had. Yet in this kind of faithful obedience, Peter will glorify God (v. 19), just as Jesus' own crucifixion was, against all appearances, the supreme moment of glorification. In all of this, Jesus asks Peter—and he would ask us too—nothing more, but nothing less, than to 'follow me' (v. 19), as one final time the story goes back to the beginning and to that first time when Peter was commissioned: 'Follow me.'

In a sense, everything has changed since then; but in another sense nothing has changed—the call remains the same. The call to martyrdom that Peter, and other disciples, will receive is not a separate call from the original one to follow; not an extra stage added on later. When Jesus calls us to take up our crosses, to deny ourselves, and to follow him (Mark 8:34), *at that point* our lives as we know them are over, because it is only those who do not hold on to their lives who will ever save them. The trouble is that, without a sense of the true cost of discipleship, so many of us never truly hand over our lives to Jesus in the first place. Christianity is all too often for us a 'lifestyle accessory' rather than a dying and a rising in the path of our Master. When the going gets tough, we sometimes try to save the very life that we are called to lose, and we still cling on to the world, at the cost of our souls.

Today, again, Jesus invites us to follow him, wherever that may lead (Revelation 14:4b).

Forgiveness, restoration and us

Archbishop Desmond Tutu said: 'True forgiveness deals with the past, all of the past, to make the future possible.'[72] The first step towards forgiveness is to allow the truth of the past to come out into the open if there is to be any hope of travelling unburdened into the future.

If anyone should know this, it is Desmond Tutu. After the abolition of apartheid in South Africa, Archbishop Tutu chaired the Truth and Reconciliation Commission which was set up in 1995 to pursue restorative justice and to seek to heal the wounds of the nation. The commission was empowered to grant amnesty to those who committed abuses during the apartheid era, as long as the crimes were politically motivated, proportionate, and there was full disclosure by the person seeking amnesty. The past does not simply go away, either on a political stage or at a personal level. Things that remain pushed under the carpet can later become things that we all trip over. Wounds that get pushed deeper down will always resurface at some point or other. We must allow the truth about ourselves to be told and to live with it.

One of the reasons that we can struggle with telling the

truth about ourselves is that we live in a society 'that runs on the delusion of the importance of success'.[73] 'Bigger and better' is so often how we are taught to judge the world. In the words we reflected on at the end of Chapter 3, our world runs precisely on 'pre-eminence, prosperity, position, promotions, plaudits [and] popularity'. There is the constant pressure 'to be right, first, tops, recognised, praised, regarded [and] rewarded'; yet success, contrary to appearances, can be very dangerous. What seems like the obvious goal for everyone to aim for can actually be deeply problematic. After all, Jesus himself said that it was perfectly possible to gain the whole world—'success' on the ultimate scale—and at the same time, to lose your soul (Mark 8:36). Jesus was willing to 'fail' in the eyes of the world—to lose his life in order that he might gain it again.

Success is always, at best, relative. We can only define ourselves as successful, or not, when we compare ourselves against other people. While there may always be those against whom we decide that we are more successful, there will be those against whom we come up short by comparison. Furthermore, success is only ever temporary. We may be successful for a season, but the successes of today can be quickly forgotten. No one can be successful for ever: our minds will eventually slow down and our bodies will eventually fail us. Despite all this, though, the lure of success can be difficult to resist. Like a drug, it can keep us wanting just one more fix after another.

Jesus knew very well the dangers of success. Not only did he warn his disciples of its perils but, before this, he resisted its allure. In his temptation by the devil in the wilderness, Jesus not only refused to be controlled by his desires, but he also resisted the attractions of both critical popularity and personal ambition (Matthew 4:1–11). For me, this can only be because, far above the voice of the tempter, Jesus was tuned in to the voice of the Father. At his baptism, he heard that voice speaking words of affirmation to him: 'This is my Son whom I love; with him I am well pleased' (Matthew 3:17). This voice spoke before Jesus had 'achieved' anything. It was not conditional on anything but was based solely on the unconditional love of God. Jesus knew his core identity, as the beloved of the Father, and he never stopped living out of that. Other voices came and went, inviting him to define himself by other means and in other ways; yet they could never draw him away from the voice of the Father that was always speaking to him, affirming him, properly locating him.

Because Jesus, as the beloved Son, has modelled the example and, by his life, death and resurrection, made the way for us to follow, we, in him, can choose to do that. In the words of Brennan Manning: 'Define yourself radically as one beloved by God. This is the true self. Every other identity is illusion.'[74] This was the lesson that Peter had to learn. The account of Peter's denial can only have come from Peter himself, who with extraordinary openness and vulnerability was able to reveal his own weakness and failure. Surely it was only his rootedness in his identity as one loved and forgiven by the Father that enabled him to be so open.

The first step towards forgiveness is to come clean; to admit where we are; to not be so driven by our desire for 'success' that we are unable to admit our failure. Having said that, something else is required as well. Both Peter and Judas failed Jesus—one by denying Jesus and the other by betraying him. We could quibble over the relative merits of each act but the truth is that both disciples failed their teacher in the most dramatic of ways—apostasy and treachery. Furthermore, both regretted what they had done. Both expressed great remorse. Both came clean. Both wished they could undo their actions. And yet, while one went on to become the foundational leader of the early church—the rock on which Jesus said he would build his church—the other committed suicide. What was the difference between them? In the words of Paul to the Corinthians, though they may look similar on the surface, there is a vast difference between 'godly grief' and 'worldly grief'. 'For godly grief produces a repentance that leads to salvation and brings no regret, but worldly grief produces death' (2 Corinthians 7:10, NRSV). What counts is not what is going on at the surface, but rather what is taking place deeper down.

This is where Peter in his failure is, in fact, a wonderful model to us in ours. Not only was he able to admit his failure, he was also able to accept it—together with the forgiveness that would flow from that acceptance. Many of us may be able to come clean about who we are and what we have done, but be unable to live with the shame and the scandal of it all. We fall into self-pity, and the weight of our failure is simply too great for us to carry by ourselves. And, of course, it is. But then we were never meant to carry all of it by ourselves. There was a major difference between Peter and Judas regarding whom they sought out to share their burden of guilt and shame. As soon as Judas realised exactly what he had done, he brought back the 30 pieces of silver to the chief priests and the elders. He confessed his sin, but he was offered no support: 'What is that to us? That's your responsibility,' was all they said (Matthew 27:4). Judas was sent out to carry the burden by himself. He couldn't do it and so, tragically, he went out and hanged himself.

Peter was different. Clearly he could draw on the support of the other disciples. There was a level of companionship there that Judas was unable to benefit from. But Peter went a stage further even than that: he ran, or rather he swam, to Jesus. Instinctively perhaps, he knew that, if there was any hope of moving on from his failure, it could only come by throwing himself on the mercy and compassion of Jesus. So it must be with us. Before we can minister for Jesus, we must allow him to minister to us. Although the support of friends and family may be vital, it will only be as we run to Jesus with our confession of who we are and what we have done that there will be any possibility of freedom from shame and the hope of a future for us.

We can do this in the knowledge that God's love for us is vast and his grace towards us unending. As Rowan Williams said, 'The gospel will never tell us we are innocent, but it will tell us we are loved.'[75] Nothing that we do can add to this and nothing can take away from it. We spend so much of our lives experiencing conditional love from those around us—rising when we please them, but falling when we disappoint—that this can be incredibly difficult to understand. In this new world of resurrection and grace, all things have been turned on their head—or rather, they have been set the right way around again. As Jesus did, we live out of an identity in which we are the beloved of the Father—loved long before we have ever 'achieved' anything for God, and loved way after we have failed him in countless ways and means.

As the psalmist says, 'For his unfailing love toward those who fear him is as great as the height of the heavens above the earth. He has removed our sins as far from us as the east is from the west' (Psalm 103:11–12, NLT). East and west have no fixed coordinates, hence the distance between them is infinite. In the same way, God's forgiveness for us is infinite, unending, unfathomable. We will never scale its heights nor plumb its depths. ''Tis mystery all', as Charles Wesley wrote in one of his most famous hymns. God has forgiven us, so who are we to be unable to forgive ourselves? God, in Christ, beckons us on to a new hope and a new future.

'True forgiveness deals with the past, all of the past, to make the future possible.'[76] Freedom and a future are precisely what Peter receives following his encounter with the risen Christ. Not only is his past forgiven but he is commissioned for a new future. He will share in the shepherding ministry of the good shepherd himself, and eventually come to lose his life in the same way that Jesus did. He will be the rock on which Jesus will build his church. Yet importantly:

His qualification to lead the new Christian community is not his successes, such as the time he alone recognises exactly who Jesus is [Mark 8:29], nor his failures, for we would all equally qualify there, but his response to his failures. His qualification to share the ministry of a 'failed' Messiah is that he has been drawn deeply into the mystery of failure and through it he has known God's love and forgiveness.[77]

Peter is a 'forgiven failure' and that is enough for God to be able to take him and use him. We can never serve God out of our own qualifications but only out of an acknowledgement of his overwhelming grace. Paul, too, came to realise that God has placed his grace in ordinary vessels like us in the same way that people in the first century would keep their treasure in jars of clay. Who would imagine that something so valuable would be entrusted inside something so ordinary? And all of this is 'so that it may be made clear that this extraordinary power belongs to God and does not come from us' (2 Corinthians 4:7, NRSV). Hudson Taylor, the founder of the China Inland Mission, wrote these words: 'All God's giants have been weak men and women, who did great things for God because they reckoned on His being with them.'[78]

However, this is so counterintuitive to the ways of our world that it can be a hard lesson for us to learn. Naturally, many of us quite like success—not necessarily because of the acclaim it might bring, or even out of any personal ambition, but perhaps because we just like to do things well. We try to work hard and set high standards for ourselves, and surely to work in this way for the kingdom of God can only be a good thing? Yet we need to learn that it is not always a good thing. Not when our hard work and our high standards cause us to lose a sense of God as our source and the one on whom we are wholly dependent: 'Apart from me you can do nothing,' said Jesus (John 15:5). Like Peter, we can fall into an overly high opinion of ourselves and all that we think we might be capable of for Jesus (Matthew 26:33). Perversely, our desire for success—even perfection—for the kingdom can make us afraid to risk something bold for God in case we get it wrong. Perfectionists like me, and all who might be seduced by the allure of success, need to be saved. And the most likely thing that God will use to save us is, in fact, for us to fail at something, but to 'fail well'.

By failing well, I mean to fail; to come to a real sense of oneself as weaker than we previously thought; and then to throw ourselves on to Jesus for forgiveness and future dependence—just as Peter did. In an interview for Catalyst Live 2014, a conference of the Baptist Missionary Society, Fr Richard Rohr commented on how he was aware of the dangers of success—in his case, the 'problem' of becoming well known and of having people listening to him in a way that he came to expect. His response has been to pray for a daily humiliation—at least one thing that doesn't go his way each day—and then to watch his reaction to it in order to see how honest and humble he is about himself. He observes that it isn't hard to stay humble if only we will be honest about ourselves.

Elsewhere Rohr has said:

Once we reach the age of thirty, success has nothing to teach us. Success is fun and rewarding, but we don't learn anything new from it. It's not a bad friend; it's just a lousy teacher. The only thing that can teach us, that can get through to us and profoundly change us, is suffering, failure, loss and wounds.[79]

Failure, then, can actually be a gift. It causes us to drop the pretence and see ourselves for who we really are. It humbles us and forces us to consider just how dependent we are on God. As Oswald Chambers said: 'Complete weakness and dependence will always be the occasion for the Spirit of God to manifest His power.'[80] Furthermore, it should give us a deep compassion for others in their failings. Be wary of the leader who has never failed: invariably, they will be a harsh taskmaster. Or, as John Wimber used to say, 'never trust a leader without a limp'.[81] Peter would 'walk with a limp' for the rest of his days, right up until the day that he gave his life for Christ. Yet there can be no doubt that this failed but forgiven Peter was a far more powerful rock on which to build the church than the blustering, success-driven one. God was surely far more able to use and to mould him because of the awareness he now had of his weakness. Furthermore, there could be no pretence among the people he led as to what he was capable of.

I love the fact that such stories are never airbrushed in the Bible, but rather stand as a testament to weak and failing people brought to great use in the hands of a powerful and gracious God. The Christian life is one of 'downward mobility', and it was at the bottom that Peter came to find his place and his identity in the love and forgiveness of Jesus. Maybe this is where we need to encounter the risen Christ afresh too.

Pause and reflect: Prayer of confession and absolution

'Before we can begin to see the cross as something done for us, we have to see it as something done by us.' [82] Repentance and confession always prefigure faith and worship. In the same way, before we can ever minister for Jesus, we must allow him to minister his forgiveness to us.

The following is a prayer of confession:

Lord God, I need to tell you that I do not always get things right.
The things that I think, that I say, that I do.
I know that you already know this,
but sometimes I find it hard to admit it to myself, let alone to you.
Forgive me, and have mercy upon me;
meet me at the bottom, and raise me to new life in you.
Amen.

However, the goal of admitting our failings before God is that we might receive the forgiveness that flows from the heart of God. So, may we hear in these words the freedom that God gives us, and the hope that he restores us to:

May the Father grant forgiveness to you;
may the Son pour out his love upon you;
may the Spirit bring his freedom to you;
this day, and always.
Amen.

Discussion questions

- What aspect of Peter's personality do you most appreciate?
- What strikes you most about the way in which Jesus restored Peter?
- Why do you think we struggle with the topic of forgiveness so much today?
- How well do you think the church today navigates the issues around success and failure?
- Where have you personally known God's grace and forgiveness at work in your own failure?

Chapter 7

The Disciples: the Great Commission

They follow the Lamb wherever he goes. (Revelation 14:4)

Following Jesus is simple, but not easy. (Mother Teresa)

In encountering the risen Christ, Mary's sadness was turned to hope. For Thomas, seeing the resurrected Jesus transformed his doubt into confirmed faith. The disciples were locked in the upper room out of fear, but beholding Jesus and receiving the Holy Spirit would, over time, see them move out to tell the good news to others in fullness of confidence. Cleopas and Mary were downcast, with dreams that had shattered around them, but encountering the risen Jesus through word and meal opened up a whole new beginning for them. And for Peter, a post-breakfast encounter would see his sense of failure replaced by a restored vocation to serve the resurrected Lord Jesus.

What each of these encounters have in common—besides the person who is being encountered and the thread of disorientation, reimagination and transformation that runs through all of them—is the sense that they *all* result in people being sent out to tell others of Jesus and all that he has done. An encounter with the risen Christ *always* results in a fresh commission not only to know him deeply for oneself, but also to make him known to others. The good news of the resurrection simply cannot be contained. For this reason, we finish by looking at what has commonly been called the 'great commission'.

Then the eleven disciples went to Galilee, to the mountain where Jesus had told them to go. When they saw him, they worshipped him; but some doubted. Then Jesus came to them and said, 'All authority in heaven and on earth has been given to me. Therefore go and make disciples of all nations, baptising them in the name of the Father and of the Son and of the Holy Spirit, and teaching them to obey everything I have commanded you. And surely I am with you always, to the very end of the age.' (Matthew 28:16–20)

The eleven disciples (Judas has gone by this time) went to the mountain in Galilee where Jesus had told them to go. Fascinatingly, we are told that, even though they worshipped him when they saw him, still 'some doubted'. Clearly Thomas was not the only 'doubter' among the disciples. It is a reminder again that, for disciples then and now, it can take some time to get up to speed with all that it means to follow Jesus. Matthew 28:16–20 is a passage usually familiar to so many in the church, yet familiarity can sometimes lead us to miss things and be unable to see fresh revelation. As the ancient Greek philosopher Epictetus reminds us, 'It is impossible to begin to learn that which one thinks one already knows.'

Command 1: Go!

The first command given by Jesus is to 'go'. This is a moment to parallel the entry of Joshua and the people of Israel into the promised land. In the same way, the disciples of Jesus— then and now—are sent out into all the world, which, by his cross and resurrection, has become the new promised land. Jesus is Lord and so all is claimed for him, not just one narrow strip in the Middle East but the entire cosmos.

Such a command has been the inspiration for many to leave their own country and travel to places around the world in order to share the good news of Jesus Christ. And it is of no small note that, increasingly, it is to the West—to countries like our own—that many people are being sent on mission. We must be humble and receptive to everything that God would do in our day. Yet, whether we are called abroad or not, the call to go, the commission of being sent, applies to all who follow Jesus. Just as we gather together to worship in community each week, so we are scattered and sent out: 'Go in peace to love and serve the Lord', in the concluding words of the Holy Communion service. Our mission most normally will consist of living well and sharing Christ as the opportunity arises with friends, family, neighbours and colleagues, for example. If we cannot live out our faith in these spheres, then we are saying that Christianity has nothing to do with the overwhelming majority of our lives. As Augustine of Hippo said: 'Pay special regard to those who by the accidents of time or place or circumstances are brought into closer connection with you.'[83] The Imagine Project from London Institute for Contemporary Christianity is but one excellent resource that seeks to mobilise the church to make disciples from Monday to Saturday, as well as on Sunday.[84]

Command 2: Make disciples!

The central command in this passage is to 'make disciples': this is the very purpose of 'going'.

The point has been well made over many years now, but remains valid nonetheless, that the command is not to make 'converts' but rather to make 'disciples'. Discipleship is the process of becoming like Jesus, of living my life as he would live it. It speaks of a journey in growth and maturity, holiness and right living. Thus, Hebrews 5:12–14 speaks of maturity as moving from milk to solid food; Ephesians 4:12–15 of journeying from the fragility of the infant, blown around, to the solidity of the mature; Colossians 2:10 speaks of being 'brought to fullness', and 2 Corinthians 3:18 of being 'transformed into his likeness'. We can become so obsessed with the numbers game in the church, not least when we perceive those numbers to be shrinking. However, Dallas Willard is surely right when he says, 'Instead of counting Christians, we need to weigh them.'[85] Conversion, or making the decision to follow Christ, is merely the beginning of a journey that will last for the rest of our lives—it is certainly not the immediate destination. The one who thinks they are finished *is* finished. In truth, we are always unfinished, always on our way, always growing in maturity, until the appearing of Christ to make us like him at last.

Dallas Willard famously said that discipleship is the 'great omission from the Great Commission'.[86] Certainly this was the surprise finding of the 2004 REVEAL survey conducted by Willow Creek Church. Willow Creek is a megachurch in Chicago, famous for its 'seeker sensitive' services which have led to so many people becoming Christians. The church wanted to evaluate how and where people were growing in maturity in Christ as disciples. However, they were shocked by the findings, which showed that, for the most part, people weren't growing in this way. In spite of the millions of dollars in their budget, they were making converts but they weren't making disciples, as instructed by the great commission. The leadership of the church publicly repented and changed the way that mission and ministry would be led into the future.

The challenge is whether we are bold enough to ask the same questions of our own churches, and humble enough to admit it when the results come back to tell us something similar. We must be aware that the surrounding culture is not neutral; if we are not discipling effectively those within our churches, then we can be sure that mainstream culture will.

Part of the problem with the church has been an understanding of the gospel as primarily concerned with where people spend their afterlife—'Information for Evacuation' as some have called it. As a result, the main focus has been on 'how to be saved', with the message of the Bible reduced to 'Four Spiritual Laws' or 'Four Steps'. And yet the goal, as we saw in Chapter 2, is not to evacuate the earth to heaven, but rather to see God's kingdom come on earth as in heaven. The focus on salvation in the afterlife has often come at the cost of obedience in the present life. Eternal salvation has been presented as essential, but present obedience as almost optional. Jesus is seen primarily as our Saviour but only voluntarily as Lord. The result has been the creation of what Willard memorably called 'vampire Christians'[87]—those who only want Jesus for his blood; who wish to be saved by him but not to follow him in obedience or to become more like him.

Yet, discipleship is a vocation that demands a high commitment. It was Jesus himself who said, 'Whoever wants to be my disciple must deny themselves, take up their cross and follow me' (Matthew 16:24), and also 'Those of you who do not give up everything you have cannot be my disciples' (Luke 14:33). Christians in the West have a great deal to learn from our brothers and sisters around the world with regard to the cost of discipleship. In February 2015, a video emerged showing the beheadings of 21 Egyptian Christians who had been kidnapped by Islamic State militants in Libya. All 21 beheaded Egyptian Christians were given the opportunity to convert to Islam. They chose not to. As they were killed, each called out, 'Jesus is Lord.' They understood what it ultimately means to be a disciple of Jesus Christ. Similarly, the largest branch of the Mothers' Union in the world at present is in Iraq. One of the questions asked of mothers when they wish for their children to be baptised is, 'Do you want to become a martyr?' My current practice of preparing people for baptism does not include this question, but maybe it should! After all, what is baptism if not an invitation to die to the world and to rise to new life in Christ?

These stories contrast greatly with some of the overly 'seeker sensitive' models of evangelism that have been tried over recent years. The danger of lowering the bar in this way is that what you win people *with* is what you win them *to*. Evangelism and discipleship cannot be separated into two separate entities in the way that perhaps they sometimes are. The danger of a low bar in a consumer society is that you win people to a model of Christianity as lifestyle accessory. It is a bolt-on to the rest of my life, rather than something which puts the whole of my life under scrutiny. It can all too easily be 'cheap grace'[88] with Jesus as Saviour but never really as Lord.

Commands 3 and 4: Baptise and teach them!

As part of this demanding vocation to become Jesus' disciples, there comes the instruction to baptise disciples in the name of the Father, the Son and the Holy Spirit, and to teach them to obey everything that Jesus has commanded.

It is fascinating to compare the approaches of the contemporary church in these areas with those in the early centuries of Christianity. In those early centuries, baptism was not something that anyone had a 'right' to; rather, catechumens—those who wished to be baptised and to become a part of the church—had to prove their adherence to Jesus and their commitment to his Way before being accepted as part of the church. They would be thoroughly assessed through a rigorous discipleship process, taken under the wing of a mentor, and obliged to live out the ethics of the Sermon on the Mount. It could be up to four years before they were allowed to hear and respond to the gospel and so to become part of the community of faith. Such an approach was the very antithesis of seeker sensitive—there was no 'sinner's prayer' in sight—yet the church grew explosively in these years. In the West, we are often so concerned with the numbers game, yet a small band of disciples is far more useful in effecting the mission of God than crowds of religious consumers.

One of the most interesting people currently writing about baptism and catechism (the instruction and discipling that catechumens received) is the Anabaptist writer and practitioner Alan Kreider.[89] He notes that baptism plays a central role in the church when the church is marginalised and under pressure—for example, in the first few centuries after Christ as well as today in places like China. Baptism withers, both theologically and practically, he says, when Christianity becomes 'established' and part of the structure of society, as happened in the West after the fourth century. One can chart the weakening of baptismal ritual across the centuries in the fact that fonts become smaller and the use of water more restricted, such that baptism becomes 'dry cleaning'! Furthermore, when baptism is socially acceptable and comfortable, baptismal teaching and preparation become truncated—lacking in-depth preparation for living a counter-cultural life of faith. However, for Kreider, the good news is that, as the church takes its place on the margins again, baptismal renewal is taking place in our time.

It is no mistake that in the great commission, Jesus places baptism and teaching as essential ingredients in the entry process to the lifelong journey of discipleship. Such a relationship is being recovered today and Kreider argues that we must raise the bar in how we instruct candidates for baptism—and, by implication, how we instruct and disciple all Christians. His proposed curriculum may seem demanding (and it certainly is!) but so was Christ's call to his first disciples to leave *everything* in order to follow him. Where such instruction comes—before baptism, after it, or a little bit of both—is not the main issue; the main issue is to make disciples. More specifically, it is to make disciples who will themselves make disciples, and so on.

Kreider's 'Twelve Steps' curriculum covers the following elements:

1. Experiences of God: a personal knowledge that God is real and loves them.
2. The story of God: articulating the story of scripture from creation to new creation.
3. Missional issues in the congregation: understanding cultural context and what it means to live as a Christian.
4. Classic areas of addiction: for example, money, sex and power.
5. Personal problem areas: understanding and moving beyond personal coping mechanisms and defences.

6. Christian cultural critique: appreciating the graced and disgraced aspects of the world around us.
7. Prayer: teaching candidates to pray.
8. Basic Bible texts: memorising key verses from scripture.
9. Fundamental beliefs: learning the core convictions of the church.
10. Christian articulacy: being able to give 'an account of the hope that is in you' (1 Peter 3:15, NRSV).
11. Personal questions: the opportunity to ask any difficult and searching questions that candidates may have.
12. The church's practices: teaching about the distinctiveness of Christian worship and practice.

How should we teach people? Instruction, imitation and immersion

Discipleship is fundamentally about relationship—a living relationship, of course, with the living God, made possible through encountering the risen Christ in the power of the Spirit, but also a relationship in partnership and community with others. Ideally, we should each be intentionally discipled by at least one person, and we should each be intentionally discipling at least one person ourselves. In the Gospels and the book of Acts, the language of 'discipleship' is explicitly used, referring to the relationship that a Jewish rabbi would have with his disciples. As the gospel spreads out into the Greco-Roman world, this explicit terminology of 'discipleship' disappears, but the concept of growth and maturity that underlies it certainly does not. Instead, Paul seeks to use an analogy that would make more sense to the people in that culture, drawn from the parent–child relationship.

I am not writing this to make you ashamed, but to admonish you as my beloved children. For though you might have ten thousand guardians in Christ, you do not have many fathers. Indeed, in Christ Jesus I became your father through the gospel. I appeal to you, then, be imitators of me. For this reason I sent you Timothy, who is my beloved and faithful child in the Lord, to remind you of my ways in Christ Jesus, as I teach them everywhere in every church. (1 Corinthians 4:14–17, NRSV)[90]

Three dynamics—of instruction, imitation and immersion—sum up the fullness of how we learn and how we need to teach within a discipling relationship.[91] They describe what Jesus did, what Paul practised, and what we urgently need to recover today.

Jesus certainly *instructed* his disciples in many things. In Matthew's Gospel, 'teaching them to obey everything I have commanded you' (Matthew 28:20) must be seen to refer, in the first instance, to the five blocks of teaching that Jesus gives within the Gospel. These concern ethical teaching from the Sermon on the Mount (chs. 5—7), missional teaching (ch. 10), parabolic teaching about the kingdom (ch. 13), ecclesial teaching about life within the community of the church (ch. 18), and eschatological teaching about the 'end times' (chs. 23–25). Similarly Paul's letters bear tribute to the teaching of this sort that he brought to the early Christians with whom he was in relationship. Today as Christians we have instruction in abundance—sermons, small group notes, podcasts, books, conferences and events. There has never been a time where there has been greater access to this sort of material. Instruction is good and non-negotiable but, by itself, it isn't enough. We all need to see the instruction lived out in real flesh and blood. Hence the importance of *imitation*.

Human beings innately copy the patterns and behaviours of one another. During a Communion service recently, we were anointed with oil as a sign of God's commissioning of all people to minister for him in our ordinary and everyday lives. Having already given them the bread and wine, the idea was that we would make a sign of the cross on the palm of people's hands. In one group of people, the first person misunderstood the instruction and turned their hands palms down, instead of palms up. As I looked across the line, it was like dominoes falling as suddenly everyone else copied this person and did the same with their hands. We instinctively look to imitate one another. It was for this reason that the disciples saw something different about the way that Jesus was praying and wanted to learn from it: 'teach us to pray' (Luke 11:1). Imitation and instruction were combined. Paul's practice to those who followed him was to say, 'Imitate me' (1 Corinthians 4:16), just as he was imitating Christ (11:1). At first sight, this might strike us as somewhat arrogant, but it is merely the way in which discipleship—together with so much human learning—takes place.

This is not to say that Paul was perfect, nor that mentors today need to be perfect. We don't need perfect examples, just living ones. Crucially, imitation relies on access to the disciples or mentor. An instruction-based approach can be done from a distance, but imitation relies on relationship and access to the person doing the discipling. This was the model of Paul to the Thessalonians: 'Because we loved you so much, we were delighted to share with you not only the gospel of God but our lives as well' (1 Thessalonians 2:8).

The goal of both instruction and imitation is the empowering of people to grow in maturity and confidence, and so be able to live out what has been both taught and modelled.

So often, our ways of learning leave us tied to 'experts' and disempowered to put things into practice for ourselves. Jesus not only told and showed his disciples what to do, but he also involved them in his mission. Having let them observe his own ministry, Jesus sends out first the Twelve and then the Seventy-two. Imitation and instruction lead to *immersion*. In the same way, a foreign language student may study the textbooks and copy the accent of their teacher, but eventually will need to go to a place where that language is spoken and learn by soaking it up. The goal is innovation— the ability to be creatively original themselves. This is what the disciples eventually became after Pentecost—able to innovate in mission, having been instructed by Jesus, having imitated Jesus' ministry, and having been immersed in their own practice.

From the 2004 Willow Creek REVEAL report mentioned earlier, Willow Creek leaders concluded that Bible study, prayer, discipleship and missional community were all practices that must be instilled into people, to make them depend on God for growth. They admitted that not enough of their efforts had been given towards helping people become 'self-starters' in these critical areas—namely, the basic spiritual disciplines and practices of the church throughout the ages. All this is to say that at Willow Creek there had been plenty of instruction, perhaps not sufficient opportunity for imitation, but certainly not nearly enough focus on immersion. The result was a lack of innovation in those who should have been discipled. They were unable to be self-starters: they were still immature with high levels of dependence on the 'experts', rather than becoming confident in those areas themselves and then able to disciple others.

Disorientation, reimagination and transformation today

In a changing cultural context of post-Christendom, post-modernity, and the rest, there is a great deal of *disorientation* taking place in the church at present. Our experience can often feel like that of the exiles of Judah in Babylon after 587BC, the year which marked the fall of Jerusalem and the destruction of the temple. In a situation of exile, the treasured symbols of a people—be they temples or crucifix necklaces—are not respected by the surrounding dominant culture, while central stories ('metanarratives') are not shared by them either. If we need any convincing that the world around us has shifted, stories like the following need to be heard:

> *In a London school a teenager with no church connections hears the Christmas story for the first time. His teacher tells it well and he is fascinated by this amazing story. Risking his friends' mockery, after the lesson he thanks her for the story. One thing had disturbed him, so he asks: 'Why did they give the baby a swear-word for his name?'*[92]

Another such comment comes out of the debate over whether supermarkets should stock 'The Real Easter Egg' at Easter time, which features Christian crosses and a leaflet that explains the story of the resurrection. In such a context, one of the supermarkets' buyers is reported to have said: 'What has Easter got to do with the church?'[93]

In such a context, it can feel as if we have lost the known world of the past, leaving us uncertain of what the future will look like, with only marginality to hold on to in the present. Two false choices that 'exiles' often fall into are either denial or despair—either a refusal to accept that the world around us has really changed or a sinking desperation when we realise that it has. In this context, the words of Jeremiah 29 might speak to us afresh. Far from denying reality or despairing of it, we are called to settle into it because, against all the evidence, God has plans to prosper and not to harm us, to give us a hope and a future.

This is neither a call for withdrawal from the surrounding culture nor a compromise with it, but instead a seeking of its peace, or *shalom* (that word again from Chapter 3) because in its flourishing may lie our flourishing. And for us today, post-Easter, we know that God is the God of resurrection. Lesslie Newbigin, the great missionary and church leader referred to in Chapter 3, was once asked whether, looking to the future of the church as it suffered present decline, he was either an optimist or a pessimist. His answer was amazing. He said, 'I'm neither optimistic nor pessimistic. Jesus Christ is risen from the dead.' As Christians, we are always prisoners of hope.

The truth is that the church, historically and globally, has been in a position similar to ours before. In 1776, Voltaire, the French Enlightenment writer, historian and philosopher famous, among other things, for his attacks on the church, confidently predicted that '100 years from my day, there will not be a Bible in the earth'. Clearly he was no prophet! However, far more amusing is the fact that 100 years from his day, Voltaire's house had, in fact, become a Bible factory. There is certainly a powerful argument to be made that Christians save their best worship and witness for when they are on the margins of society—not least because the disorientation of the situation inevitably causes a *reimagination* within the church of what it means to be a disciple of Christ. Suddenly issues that were hazy when the church was at the centre—such as the cost of discipleship—come into sharp focus as the church finds itself in a more marginal context. Furthermore, new ways of church planting and church growth are imagined where previously there was little institutional appetite for such initiatives. It is, therefore, of no surprise, but of deep promise, that there is such a great reimagination taking place at the moment around future shapes of church—whether fresh expressions, church plants or church revitalisations.[94]

In a time of disorientation and reimagination, the church must be thrown into a humble dependence on God in prayer. In 1997, there was a *Sunday Telegraph* article about the decline of the church which ran under the headline: 'The Church On Its Knees!' If only that were more the case. Kneeling is the forgotten posture in contemporary worship— perhaps a sign that we've become too comfortable, too familiar, before God. In 1888, a pioneer missionary felt called to North Honan, considered one of the most anti-foreign and dangerous parts of China. Hudson Taylor, founder of the China Inland Mission, wrote to him. One of the things he wrote was, 'Brother, if you would enter that province, you must go forward on your knees.' Increasingly we are not so much reviving latent faith in people as re-evangelising a nation. 'Evangelising' or 'fossilising' are the two futures for the church. We must go forward on our knees.

As we reimagine the church in our day, we dream of its transformation. True disciples of Christ stand out from the people around them. They exhibit the fruits of the Spirit— love, joy, peace, patience, kindness, goodness, faithfulness, gentleness, self-control—in a surrounding culture that so often manifests hatred, despair, violence, restlessness, ruth-lessness, greed, infidelity, harshness and impulsiveness. Their holiness is the inner heart of their mission. They are those who have encountered Jesus—the surprising, unpredictable Jesus—and whose lives have been completely thrown off course as a result, just as Saul's was. They are those whose lives have had to be completely reimagined in the light of their encounter; who, having found treasure hidden in a field, have gone and sold all they had in order to buy that field (Matthew 13:44). And they are formed into the image of Christ 'from one degree of glory to another' (2 Corinthians 3:18, NRSV). Their sadnesses are being overwhelmed by hope; their fears consumed by confidence; their doubts grown into faith confirmed; their shattered dreams replaced by new beginnings; and their failures covered by forgiveness and restoration.

Authority and presence

Jesus' command in the great commission is to 'go', to 'make disciples', to 'baptise' and to 'teach'. These commands (vv. 19–20) are only possible because of the promises that surround them (vv. 18, 20). Jesus' disciples are to obey him in these commands in the knowledge, first of all, that all authority in heaven and earth belongs to him, as a result of his resurrection. All other powers have been defeated; Christ sits as Lord of all. We make disciples, we baptise, we teach, not in our own authority but only in his. Second, we do these things in the world enveloped by his presence. As A.W. Tozer said: 'We need never to shout across the spaces to an absent God. He is nearer than our own soul. Closer than our most secret thoughts.'[95] Thus, Matthew's Gospel starts with the birth of Jesus, Emmanuel, God-With-Us, and it ends with the promise that 'I am with you always, to the very end of the age' (v. 20).

This presence comes by the gift of the Spirit, poured out on the church at Pentecost. This same Spirit renews and equips the church for its tasks, which constitute a partnering with God for the healing of the world and the coming of his kingdom. This is the same Spirit that raised Christ from the dead, and the Spirit of God will not stop in his work in the world until all that is dead has been brought to life and God's new creation has come into being. Being present with the Spirit in the places where there is the stench of death—of a decaying old creation—may not always be comfortable; but such places are precisely where the church is called to be, in order that the life of the resurrection—the vitality of the new creation—may come to fruition. The words of General William Booth, spoken many years ago to those in the Salvation Army, remain challenging to all of us, all these years later:

You have enjoyed yourself in Christianity long enough. You have had pleasant feelings, pleasant songs, pleasant meetings, and pleasant prospects. There has been much of human happiness, much clapping of hands and shouting of praises, very much of heaven on earth. Now then, go to God and tell Him you are prepared as much as necessary to turn your back upon it all, and that you are willing to spend the rest of your days struggling in the midst of these perishing multitudes, whatever it may cost you.[96]

Veni, Sancte Spiritus! Come, Holy Spirit!

Pause and reflect: a prayer of abandonment

At the end of this book—as we reflect on all that Easter means, and are reminded of our need of the Spirit for the tasks that we have been given—we can meditate on, and pray, the following words of commitment to God:

Father,
I abandon myself into your hands;
do with me what you will.
Whatever you may do, I thank you:
I am ready for all, I accept all.
Let only your will be done in me,
and in all your creatures.
I wish no more than this, O Lord.

Into your hands I commend my soul;
I offer it to you
with all the love of my heart,
for I love you, Lord,
and so need to give myself,
to surrender myself into your hands,
without reserve,
and with boundless confidence,
for you are my Father.
CHARLES DE FOUCAULD

Discussion questions

- Where are you called to 'go' to? How would you define your primary mission field?
- How significant a place does baptism have in your understanding of the great commission?

- How effective do you think teaching and learning are in the church today? What specific things could make them better?
- How do you feel about the changing culture that faces the church in our society today?
- What 'disorientation', 'reimagination' and 'transformation' do you feel that God is doing in you at present?

Pentecost

I want to feel that first breath of life
as Christ's disciples felt it
when the Spirit breathed into them
and they received that initial inhalation
of truth.

The naked fruit of life
peeled back within their mouths,
oriented into air.

Capillaries expanded,
delivered doses
of oxygenated ascendance
into every low, shadowed
space within them
followed by one single
exalted exhalation—
death-groan of death itself.

The hollow became hallowed.

My heart might rupture
under the pressure
of so much mercy
but I ask
that You consecrate me anyway.

The next time I contour my mouth
in some half-formed expression
let it mirror You fully
so that everything not of You
becomes a blackened coal,
and love
becomes the all-consuming flame
dancing on my lips.

R.A. WRIGHT

Notes

1 Author unknown.
2 Tom Wright, *Surprised by Hope* (SPCK, 2007), pp. 256–257.
3 See Paul Bradshaw, *Early Christian Worship* (SPCK, 2010), pp. 88–93.
4 Chaplain Mike, 'Easter: do we just not "get" it?' www.internetmonk.com/archive/55897.
5 Alvin Toffler, *Future Shock* (Random House, 1970), p. 367.
6 Tom Wright, *Paul: Fresh Perspectives* (SPCK, 2005), p. 98.
7 Source unknown.
8 From the Epistle to Diognetus, 5–6.
9 Dallas Willard, *The Divine Conspiracy: Rediscovering our hidden life in God* (William Collins, 1998), p. 36.
10 Dietrich Bonhoeffer, *The Cost of Discipleship* (SCM Press, 2001), p. 44.
11 Northumbria Community, *Celtic Daily Prayer* (Collins, 2005), pp. 191–193.
12 Reported in George Herbert, *Jacula Prudentum* (1640), No. 1006.
13 Barbara Johnson, *Splashes of Joy in the Cesspools of Life* (Thomas Nelson, 1996), p. 193.
14 See www.equalitytrust.org.uk/resources/the-spirit-level and http://thedividedocumentary.com/blog.
15 Aleksandr Solzhenitsyn, *The Gulag Archipelago 1918–1956* (HarperCollins, 1974), p. 312.
16 Howard Astin, *12½ Steps to Spiritual Health* (Monarch, 2002).
17 Thomas Merton, *Raids on the Unspeakable* (New Directions, 1966), p. 5.
18 C.S. Lewis, *Mere Christianity* (Geoffrey Bles, 1952), p. 111.
19 Jubilee+, *Investing More for the Common Good: National Church and Social Action Survey 2014*
20 See www.jubilee-plus.org/Articles/432554/Jubilee_Plus/Blog/2015/March/UNSUNG_HEROES_REACHING.aspx.
21 Words by Maltbie Davenport Babcock, 1901, alt.

22 Cited in Robert L. Short, *The Gospel According to the Dogs* (HarperCollins, 2007), p. 40.

23 Karl Barth, *Church Dogmatics* I/1, p. 247.

24 Cited in Jason Mandryk, *Operation World: The definitive prayer guide to every nation* (Biblica Europe, 2010), p. xxiii.

25 From the hymn 'Crown him with many crowns' (Matthew Bridges/Godfrey Thring).

26 Tim Dearborn, *Beyond Duty: A passion for Christ, a heart for mission* (MARC Europe, 1998), p. 2.

27 See Tom Smail, 'The Cross and the Spirit: Towards a Theology of Renewal', in Tom Smail, Andrew Walker and Nigel Wright, *Charismatic Renewal* (SPCK, 1995).

28 Smail, 'The Cross and the Spirit', in Smail, Walker and Wright, *Charismatic Renewal*, pp. 59–60.

29 Malcolm Doney and Linda Woodhead (eds), *How Healthy is the C of E?: The Church Times Health Check* (Canterbury Press, 2014).

30 Lesslie Newbigin, *Unfinished Agenda* (St Andrews Press, 1993), p. 11.

31 Cole Moreton, 'Rowan Williams: I didn't really want to be Archbishop' (*Daily Telegraph*, 27 April 2004).

32 Newbigin, *Unfinished Agenda*, p. 230.

33 Jon Kuhrt, 'Proper confidence in the gospel: the theology of Lesslie Newbigin' (2009): www.fulcrum-anglican.org.uk/articles/proper-confidence-in-the-gospel-the-theology-of-lesslie-newbigin.

34 Lesslie Newbigin, *The Open Secret* (SPCK, 1995), p. 15.

35 Jon Kuhrt, 'Proper confidence in the gospel'.

36 Michael Green, *Evangelism in the Early Church* (Eerdmans, 1970), p. 173.

37 Cited in Gerald L. Sittser, *Water from a Deep Well: Christian spirituality from early martyrs to modern missionaries* (IVP, 2010), p. 54.

38 The Imagine Project from the London Institute of Contemporary Christianity is very strong on this, particularly within the context of the workplace. There are many courses out there to teach us to be more confident in evangelism and

witness: for example, the Natural Evangelism course from the Philo Trust (www.canonjjohn.com/the-natural-evangelism-course).

39 One resource for finding out about this is the *International Bulletin for Missionary Research* (IBMR) that the Gordon Conwell Theological Seminary-based Centre for the Global Study of Christianity has produced for the past 31 years.

40 Krish Kandiah, 'The Church is growing, and here are the figures that prove it' (*Christian Today*, 5 March 2015), www.christiantoday.com/article/a.growing.church.why.we.should.focus.on.the.bigger.picture/49362.htm.

41 G.K. Chesterton, *The Everlasting Man* (Hodder & Stoughton, 1925), p. 288.

42 Quote taken from promotional video for Jonathan K. Dodson and Brad Watson, *Raised? Finding Jesus by Doubting the Resurrection* (Zondervan, 2014), www.youtube.com/watch?v=9EH0p87vDOQ.

43 See https://commons.wikimedia.org/wiki/File:Caravaggio_-_The_Incredulity_of_Saint_Thomas.jpg.

44 Greg Boyd, *Benefit of the Doubt: Breaking the idol of certainty* (Baker Books, 2013).

45 Brian McClaren, *Naked Spirituality: A life with God in twelve simple words* (Hodder & Stoughton, 2012), pp. 31–34.

46 Mike Yaconelli, *Dangerous Wonder: The adventure of childlike faith* (NavPress, 2003), p. 40.

47 Cited in 'Did Jesus really rise from the dead?' (*The Spectator*, 15 April 2006, www.spectator.co.uk/features/15157/did-jesus-really-rise-from-the-dead/) .

48 Matthew Parris, 'If Jesus did not exist, the Church would not invent him' (*The Spectator*, 22 April 2006): www.spectator.co.uk/columnists/matthew-parris/15182/if-jesus-did-not-exist-the-church-would-not-invent-him.

49 For more on this, see, among others, William Lane Craig, *Did Jesus Rise From The Dead?* (Impact 360 Institute, 2014).

50 John A.T. Robinson, *The Human Face of God* (Westminster, 1973), p. 131.

51 Brennan Manning, *The Ragamuffin Gospel: Good news for the bedraggled, beat-up, and burnt out* (Multnomah, 1990), p. 199.

52 Pete Rollins, *My Confession: I deny the resurrection*, http://peterrollins.net/2009/01/my-confession-i-deny-the-resurrection.

53 Yaconelli, *Dangerous Wonder*, pp. 40–41.

54 C.S. Lewis, *The Lion, the Witch, and the Wardrobe* (Lion Publishing, 1981), p. 182.

55 Yaconelli, *Dangerous Wonder*, p. 40.

56 Attributed to Sr Ruth Marlene Fox (1985).

57 Source unknown.

58 John 19:25. 'Clopas' is a very rare Semitic form of the Greek name 'Cleopas'.

59 Conrad Gempf, *Jesus Asked: What he wanted to know* (Zondervan, 2003), p. 23.

60 Tom Wright, *Luke For Everyone* (SPCK, 2001), p. 294.

61 Paul Ricoeur, *The Symbolism of Evil* (Beacon Press, 1967), p. 349.

62 Edward T. Hall, *The Hidden Dimension* (Anchor Books/Doubleday, 1966), pp. 113–130.

63 See, for example, www.churchofengland.org/prayer-worship/worship/texts/lectionaries.aspx.

64 www.bibleinoneyear.org.

65 See #BiOY on Twitter.

66 www.youversion.com.

67 Robin Parry, 'What the Eucharist means to me (Holy Communion as deep church)' (October 2013), http://theologicalscribbles.blogspot.co.uk/2013/10/what-eucharist-means-to-me-holy.html.

68 N.T. Wright, *Simply Jesus: Who he was, what he did, why it matters* (SPCK, 2011), p. 180.

69 St Augustine, Sermon 57 *On the Eucharist*.

70 Richard Bauckham, *The Testimony of the Beloved Disciple* (Baker Academic, 2007), pp. 271–284.

71 Tom Wright, *John for Everyone, Part 2* (SPCK, 2002), p. 161.

72 Desmond Tutu, *No Future Without Forgiveness* (Rider, 1999), p. 228.

73 Judy Hirst, *Struggling to be Holy* (DLT, 2008), p. 102.

74 Brennan Manning, *Abba's Child: The cry of the heart for intimate belonging* (NavPress, 2002), p. 60.

75 Rowan Williams, *Resurrection* (Morehouse, 1982), p. 89.

76 Desmond Tutu, *No Future Without Forgiveness*, p. 228.

77 Judy Hirst, *Struggling to be Holy*, p. 117.

78 Cited in Warren W. Wiersbe, *The Wiersbe Bible Commentary: Old Testament* (David C. Cook, 2007), p. 523.

79 See Ryan Thomas Neace, *Father Richard Rohr: Interviews with spiritual heroes* (February 2015), http://ryanthomasneace. com/2015/02/02/father-richard-rohr-interviews-with-spiritual-heroes.

80 Oswald Chambers, 5 May, in *My Utmost for His Highest* (Barbour, 2007), p. 126

81 John Wimber, 'Leaders With a Limp' in *Equipping The Saints*, Vol. 3, No. 1/Winter 1989.

82 John Stott, *The Cross of Christ* (IVP, 2006), p. 72.

83 Augustine of Hippo, *On Christian Doctrine*, Book 1, Chapter 28.

84 See www.licc.org.uk/imagine-church/; Tracey Cotterell and Neil Hudson, *Leading a Whole-Life Disciplemaking Church* (Grove, 2012); Neil Hudson, *Imagine Church* (IVP, 2012).

85 Dallas Willard and Dieter Zander, 'The Apprentices', interviewed in *Leadership* (1 July 2005).

86 Dallas Willard, *The Great Omission: Reclaiming Jesus' essential teachings on discipleship* (Monarch, 2006).

87 Willard, *The Great Omission*, p. 256.

88 Dietrich Bonhoeffer, *The Cost of Discipleship*, pp. 42–44.

89 See, for example, Alan Kreider, 'Baptism and Catechesis as Spiritual Formation', in Andrew Walker and Luke Bretherton, *Remembering Our Future: Explorations in deep church* (Paternoster, 2007), pp. 170–206.

90 See Mike Breen, 'The Great Disappearance: why the word "disciple" disappears after Acts 21 and why it matters for us today' (*Exponential*, 2013) for more on this.

91 Adapted from Mike Breen, *Building a Discipling Culture* (3DM, 2011), pp. 41–43.

92 Stuart Murray Williams, *Post-Christendom* (Paternoster, 2001), p. 1.

93 See, for example, www.christiantoday.com/article/how.did. we.fail.to.get.the.word.out.about.easter/51301.htm.

94 Regarding fresh expressions of church, see www. freshexpressions.org.uk. For one example of church planting/ church revitalisations see www.htb.org/about/related-churches.

95 A.W. Tozer, *The Pursuit of God* (Christian Publications, 1948), p. 59.

96 Sermon entitled 'Don't forget' by General Booth in 1910. Transcript can be found at www.newlifepublishing.co.uk/wp/ hot-topics/in-need-of-a-saviour.

About the author

Mark Bradford is a Church of England vicar, currently serving his curacy at Holy Trinity Church, Ripon. Before training for ordained ministry, he was a secondary school teacher in Harrogate for nine years, teaching mainly history and politics. He also worked part-time for the Oasis Trust in Leeds for three years, training and discipling 18- to 25-year-olds.

Mark loves running and, in 2014, completed the London Marathon in aid of Cancer Research. He also loves good music, good food, the beach and the sea. He is married with three young children.

Mark tweets at @mark_bradford.

Meet Jesus

A call to adventure

John Twisleton

In a world of competing philosophies, where does Jesus fit in? How far can we trust the Bible and the Church? What difference does Jesus make to our lives and our communities? Is Jesus really the be all and end all?

Meet Jesus is a lively and straightforward exploration of these and other questions, with the aim of engaging our reason, inspiring our faith and worship, deepening our fellowship and service, and bringing new depth to our witness to the world.

Each chapter ends with some practical points for actions and the book concludes with a section of discussion material for groups.

ISBN 978 1 84101 895 9   £7.99
Available from your local Christian bookshop or direct from BRF: please visit www.brfonline.org.uk.

Peter's Preaching

The message of Mark's Gospel

Jeremy Duff

As the earliest of the Gospels, Mark is arguably the foundational text of Christianity, summarising the core of Jesus' teaching. Vivid, immediate and provocative, it is in essence the preaching of Peter, Jesus' closest disciple, calling men and women to a more radical discipleship.

Peter's Preaching brings to life the content and meaning of Mark's Gospel for contemporary readers, combining the in-depth analysis of a commentary with the accessibility of Bible reading notes.Each chapter explores a key theme from Mark, covering every verse in the Gospel while also showing how the text links together as a whole. It is a valuable tool for those preaching and teaching the Bible, as well as those embarking on theological study and anyone wishing to deepen their grasp of this Gospel.

ISBN 978 0 85746 350 0   £9.99
Available from your local Christian bookshop or direct from BRF: please visit www.brfonline.org.uk.

Enjoyed

this book?

Write a review—we'd love to hear what you think.
Email: reviews@brf.org.uk

Keep up to date—receive details of our new books as they happen.
Sign up for email news and select your interest groups at:
www.brfonline.org.uk/findoutmore/

Follow us on Twitter @brfonline

By post—to receive new title information by post (UK only), complete the form below and post to: BRF Mailing Lists, 15 The Chambers, Vineyard, Abingdon, Oxfordshire, OX14 3FE

Your Details
Name _____
Address_____
_____
Town/City _____ Post Code _____
Email _____

Your Interest Groups (*Please tick as appropriate)	
☐ Advent/Lent	☐ Messy Church
☐ Bible Reading & Study	☐ Pastoral
☐ Children's Books	☐ Prayer & Spirituality
☐ Discipleship	☐ Resources for Children's Church
☐ Leadership	☐ Resources for Schools

Support your local bookshop
Ask about their new title information schemes.